Landscaping with Stone

A *Sunset* Outdoor Design & Build Guide

By Tom Wilhite and the Editors of *Sunset*

Sunset

©2010 by Time Home Entertainment Inc.
135 West 50th Street, New York, NY 10020

ISBN-13: 978-0-376-01429-0   ISBN-10: 0-376-01429-6
Library of Congress Control Number: 2009937372

10 9 8 7 6 5 4 3 2 1
First Printing December 2010. Printed in the United States of America.

OXMOOR HOUSE
VP, PUBLISHING DIRECTOR: Jim Childs
EDITORIAL DIRECTOR: Susan Payne Dobbs
BRAND MANAGER: Fonda Hitchcock
MANAGING EDITOR: Laurie S. Herr

SUNSET PUBLISHING
PRESIDENT: Barb Newton
VP, EDITOR-IN-CHIEF: Katie Tamony
CREATIVE DIRECTOR: Mia Daminato

Outdoor Design & Build Guide: *Landscaping with Stone*
CONTRIBUTORS
AUTHOR: Tom Wilhite
MANAGING EDITOR: Bob Doyle
ART DIRECTOR: Susan Scandrett
PHOTO EDITOR: Philippine Scali
PRODUCTION SPECIALIST: Linda M. Bouchard
ILLUSTRATOR: Damien Scogin
PROOFREADER: John Edmonds
INDEXER: Marjorie Joy
TECHNICAL ADVISOR: Scott Gibson
COVER PHOTO: Photography by Roger Foley; landscape design by Tom Mannion

To order additional publications, call 1-800-765-6400
For more books to enrich your life, visit **oxmoorhouse.com**
Visit Sunset online at **sunset.com**
For the most comprehensive selection of Sunset books, visit **sunsetbooks.com**
For more exciting home and garden ideas, visit **myhomeideas.com**

contents

Inspiration

Take a broad-ranging garden tour and see some of the many ways that stone can be used to enhance the landscape. From simple paths and garden walls to stylish patios complete with outdoor kitchens, and from stone pools to outdoor fireplaces, you'll find a wealth of intriguing ideas to adapt to your own setting and tastes.

How to Build

page 116

Here you'll find step-by-step instructions for a variety of basic stonework projects and techniques, along with expert tips on design, construction, and safety.

Finishing the Look

page 164

Before you shop for the stone for your new path, patio, or wall, refer to this chapter to review your options. You'll also find a sampler on garden lighting, as well as suggestions on the best plant choices to complement every type of stonework installation.

Inspiration

A beautiful garden is more than just a pleasing arrangement of plants. It needs structure to truly stir us and to be an inviting outdoor space. And there is no better or more natural material for building and decorating landscapes than stone—the very essence of the earth. Whether stone is processed into uniform blocks for walls, crushed into gravel for paths, or simply collected from a field or riverbed, its innate simplicity and unmatched durability make it the first choice for landscaping projects. Its permanence and heft accentuate the softness and fleeting beauty of nearby plants. It is also the ultimate in low-maintenance landscaping elements. In this chapter, you'll find a host of ways that stone can be used to bring structure and beauty to a garden—along with a wealth of tips on design and practical matters from *Sunset*'s landscaping experts.

Stone is a natural unifier in the garden. Here, the main flag-stone path is joined by a side path of stepping-stones and an arrangement of river boulders suggestive of a creek bed.

stepping-stone paths

LEFT: Uniform, closely spaced stepping-stones on a bed of gravel make for a path that's easy to navigate, freeing visitors (human or canine) to focus their attention on the showcase wall garden rather than on where the next step lies.

TOP RIGHT: Surrounded by a lush ground-cover carpet, these large flagstones are spaced to accommodate the gardener's gait. Their neutral color is a nice contrast to the vivid hues surrounding them.

BOTTOM RIGHT: Not all stepping-stones in a path have to be the same. Here, two runs of dark rectangular stones transition to light-colored round ones just before the whimsical path enters the lawn.

7

LEFT: Concrete stepping-stones laid in parallel lines invite side-by-side strolling across the lawn.

ABOVE: Stepping-stones offer flexibility to your garden design. This curving path can easily be moved to make more room for the hydrangeas as they grow.

design lesson

>> To make stepping-stones visually flow, place the stones so that they relate to their neighbors. Lay a straight edge of one stone against a straight edge of another, a concave edge against a convex edge.

LEFT: Paths need not march along in a straight line; here, stepping-stones meander casually around the water feature and seating area.

TOP RIGHT: When set in a lawn, stepping-stones should be flush with the soil so they don't interfere with mowing.

BOTTOM RIGHT: A stepping-stone path of flagstones curves through a tightly packed bed of river pebbles. Consider mortaring this type of path in place so that rolling pebbles don't present a hazard.

gravel paths

LEFT: The gravel in this casual path works well as both an inexpensive, attractive paving material and an excellent mulch for pathside plants that need good drainage, like the garden pinks in the foreground.

RIGHT: Formal and clean looking, a wide path of white gravel looks right at home with clipped hedges and a variety of stone landscaping features.

SUNSET ASSOCIATE GARDEN EDITOR JULIE CHAI ON

protecting indoor floors

›› Place a solid stone apron and a coarse doormat at the doorstep so gravel doesn't travel on people's shoes into the house, where it might scratch floors. Gravels smaller than ½ inch in diameter are more likely to be trapped in shoe treads.

LEFT: Versatile gravel works beautifully surrounding a modern fountain and echoing the colors of the cityscape beyond. High edging keeps gravel in bounds while giving the impression of a pond within a pond.

TOP RIGHT: Wide gravel paths surround a central meadow in this water-wise garden. The permeable surface allows rainwater to percolate into the soil rather than puddle on the surface or run off into adjacent areas.

BOTTOM RIGHT: With the crunch of gravel underfoot and the sweet smell of lavender all around, this pathway is more than just another pretty picture—it's a multisensory delight.

15

LEFT: Decomposed granite over a compacted base forms a firm, clean path surface, but without the edging of low cobbles, the path would soon begin deteriorating along its edges.

ABOVE: Good-sized stones placed closely together keep a gravel path in place and double as edging for a raised bed. The neutral hues of the path and edging are an attractive complement to the mostly green garden.

design lesson

Edgings serve an obvious practical function, but they also can be a design element. A path edged with brick has a more formal look than one edged with rough stones. For a contemporary look, consider metal edging.

flagstone paths

TOP LEFT: Flagstones make a graceful transition between a gravel driveway and an entryway, and they cut down the likelihood of gravel being tracked indoors.

TOP RIGHT: Large, light-colored flagstones, placed almost like parallel stepping-stone paths, invite side-by-side strolling across the yard.

BOTTOM: Who needs a thirsty, high-maintenance front lawn? Replace it with a winding flagstone path set in pea gravel dotted with easy-care plants.

Even a long, straight path is more interesting when paved with flagstones, whose random shapes, textured surface, and plant-filled seams nicely break up the visual line.

design lesson

» To give a flagstone path the feeling of a garden bed, allow extra space between stones and tuck low-growing flowering plants into the gaps and along the outer edges.

LEFT: For a formal-looking path that won't need weeding, lay flagstones on a concrete base and apply mortar between the joints. With this kind of foundation, you can use thinner stones, down to 1 inch thick, which weigh and cost less. Make the gaps between stones ½ to 1 inch wide and relatively uniform for the best look.

ABOVE: The pinkish hues of this Arizona flagstone path—and the soft gray green of the woolly thyme planted in and around it—are in perfect harmony with the gar- den's subdued color scheme. Flagstones generally look best laid as they are here, with their longest dimensions running across the path.

fieldstone paths

LEFT: A fieldstone path made of small local stones winds through a shady moss garden decorated with ivy, ferns, and spring-flowering bulbs. Field-stones have a more rustic look than flag-stones, with rougher surfaces and more variation in shape and color.

TOP RIGHT: Fieldstone, which can be almost any rock that wasn't quarried or collected from a riverbed or beach, is available in a wide variety of shapes and sizes. On a gentle slope like this one, large stones can be used for steps, while smaller ones fill in behind.

BOTTOM RIGHT: Pick-ing up on the sandy tones of the hills in the distance, this field-stone path fits per-fectly into its environs. Rounded stones make good edging material. If a stone has a pro-trusion that prevents a good fit or makes a high spot, don a pair of goggles and chip away with a hammer and chisel.

23

cut-stone paths

TOP LEFT: Uniformly shaped stones with smoothly mortared joints were used to create this tailored walkway through a side yard.

TOP RIGHT: Set closely together, large bluestone pavers form a path as level as a concrete sidewalk, but with more color variation and textural interest.

BOTTOM: Rough-cut slabs of various shapes and sizes were used for this rugged path. Slightly darker pebbles between the cut stones complete the primitive yet elegant look.

The colors chosen for the gate, walls, and garden furniture can all be found in the multihued Utah flagstone, which was trimmed into rectangles but left with rough edges.

cobblestone
paths

LEFT: A cobblestone path brings a feeling of antiquity to a garden, and it makes a pleasingly textured walking surface.

ABOVE: Concrete cobbles are available in a wide variety of sizes, colors, and shapes. Large and small pieces were mortared into place to form this path and simple steps.

SUNSET HEAD GARDENER
RICK LAFRENTZ ON

building cobblestone paths

➤➤ To form a stable path, cobblestones should be contained within an edging and set close together with sand-filled crevices. Many concrete cobbles have an interlocking design that makes them easy to install.

LEFT: Paths don't have to be made of a single material. Here, an edged gravel path steps up to concrete pavers set in blue river stones.

TOP RIGHT: This whimsical combination of brick and round gravel offers pleasing contrasts in color and texture.

BOTTOM RIGHT: Rough-cut stepping-stones march down the middle of a gravel-based path.

LEFT: An unusual combination of materials makes this stepped path a focal point in the garden. Bright blue flagstones and large, smooth river stones set in decomposed granite evoke water moving down the hill, tempting you to follow the course and see what lies beyond the bend.

ABOVE: Laid in a grid pattern, slabs of recycled concrete and rectangular cobbles make a nice contrast with yellow-flowered lady's-mantle and gray-leaved lamb's ears along the sides. Flaws in the concrete edges are easily concealed with low plants that spread into the path.

design lesson

» For a casual, crazy-quilt path, choose a variety of materials that are flat on one side and make your own composition. Or achieve a more conventional look with materials of the same form but different colors, such as pavers in alternating shades of gray—or of the same color but different shapes, like cut stone interspersed with bricks on edge.

pebble
paths

LEFT: Pebbles are too smooth and round to make a suitable paving if left free to roll around. But when set in concrete with their flattest side up, they create a perfectly navigable path with an interesting texture.

TOP RIGHT: Another variation on the pebble-path theme: concrete sidewalks with exposed aggregate, really just small pebbles set into the surface before the concrete dries. Here, large stones in a contrasting color grace either side of the path.

BOTTOM RIGHT: Mexican pebbles, closely set in an arrow pattern, form a narrow path in a side yard where traffic is not heavy.

driveways

TOP LEFT: Gravel driveways make a satisfying crunch when cars or bikes pull in, and big rectangular concrete pavers like these leave no doubt as to the location of the entry.

TOP RIGHT: Why leave the driveway bereft of plants? Just steer carefully to avoid the miniature garden.

BOTTOM: Durable concrete pavers set in a regular pattern are a good match for the architectural style of the house, and their subtly varied colors help mediate the starkness of a black-and-white color scheme.

Though they're often the largest feature in a front-yard landscape, driveways are usually overlooked as a potential area for beautifying a home. Here, a driveway of cut stone resembles a giant mosaic, complementing the theme of the tiled roof and colorful artwork around the entry.

simple steps

These oversized concrete steps are set with exposed aggregate chosen to match the gravel in the planting beds to either side. Nestled among the good-sized boulders are succulents, cacti, and sun-loving herbs like rosemary and thyme. The stones also make a fine place for a momentary rest.

TOP LEFT: Neatly trimmed wall stone is easy to stack into simple steps. When excavating to level the steps, mound the extra soil on either side and add soft billowing plants.

TOP RIGHT: Where there's a change in elevation, people slow down and take notice of garden features like a pot of succulents or a small but interesting boulder.

BOTTOM: These linear steps are in perfect harmony with a hillside lawn, and there's just enough space between them to allow for mowing.

TOP LEFT: Pink Arizona slabs serve as treads (where you step), and strips of the same stone face the risers (the vertical portion of stairs between the treads).

TOP RIGHT: Wall stones trimmed into rough cubes are a great fit for this laid-back vegetable patch.

BOTTOM: In a deft stroke of blending elements, the designer of these steps used stone from the surrounding walls as risers and flagstone from the upper and lower patios as treads.

A high spot in the corner of the garden is a good place for a tiny patio just large enough for a couple of chaise lounges. Twin stone orbs mark the entrance to the rustic steps.

LEFT: A formal landscape design calls for more than just a few stone steps. Generously proportioned steps of Arizona flagstone flanked by walls of trimmed stone in similar shades make a fitting entrance to this gracious patio.

TOP RIGHT: Massive granite slabs make impressive steps alongside an equally rugged-looking retaining wall. A huge trimmed boulder on the landing, partway up, completes the image of solidity.

BOTTOM RIGHT: Mirroring the terra-cotta tones of the house and a large clay pot, these roughly trimmed boulders work equally well for stairs and for the raised bed beside them. Their unevenness encourages visitors to slow down or even to pause and sit.

41

LEFT: Steps mark a transition point, and this design emphasizes that with the placement of twin pillars supporting large planters. Consider adding lighting near stairs, particularly when there are just a few steps that people might not be expecting.

ABOVE: Hefty granite boulders help anchor the hillside, and lined up along the terraced staircase, they form the perfect spot for displaying plants. The weeping orange sedge repeated on the left helps to soften the scene.

SUNSET GARDEN EDITOR
KATHLEEN NORRIS BRENZEL ON

angling up steep hills

》 For maximum drama and efficiency, run steps straight up and down the slope. For an easier climb and to draw out the journey, zigzag the steps across the slope, curving it around plants or boulders placed inside the curves.

seating areas

TOP LEFT: A gravel patio and concrete benches may not sound inviting, but add a few stylish cushions and some lightweight chairs, and you'll create a space that's both comfortable and adaptable.

TOP RIGHT: Fresh air, fire, water, and stone combine with carefully chosen plants and a luxurious chair to create an irresistible resting spot.

BOTTOM: In this back-yard, you can sit at the café table, park your-self on the capstones of the raised bed, or sprawl on the slightly inclined lawn.

What could be simpler or more appealing than a couple of mid-20th-century metal chairs on a casual stone patio?

LEFT: Easy recipe for a backyard patio: Remove a section of lawn, lay landscaping fabric, build a frame from landscaping timbers, fill with gravel, and add furnishings.

TOP RIGHT: This wide path of cut stones needed a destination to make sense from a design perspective. A brightly painted café table and chairs fit the bill nicely.

BOTTOM RIGHT: As comfortable and orderly as an indoor room, this arrangement of furniture and pots on a flagstone patio is sure to tempt visitors outdoors.

TOP LEFT: Oversized steps can do double duty as a casual seating area.

TOP RIGHT: Have a tree-shaded corner of the yard where not much will grow? Add a few flagstone stepping-stones, some small boulders for interest, and a couple of Adirondacks to create an intimate garden getaway.

BOTTOM: Sophisticated, clean lines predominate in this minimalist back patio. White stucco walls and black furniture make a striking contrast to the warmer, richer tones of wood and stone.

For the look of an outdoor living room, consider close-set stone tiles as paving. Even with a range of shapes and subtly varied hues, they proffer a tailored look.

LEFT: Maybe it's the fresh air or the novelty of the setting, but food tastes better when you dine outdoors. If you can find a spot that is somewhat removed from the house—like this charming nook reminiscent of an Italian courtyard—so much the better for the sense of adventure.

ABOVE: Formal-looking cut-stone pavers, chosen to harmonize with the walls of the house, make a smooth, stable surface for sturdy wooden chairs and a substantial table. The umbrella offers shade and a sense of enclosure and comfort, while extra seating along the perimeter—including the fun "toadstools" in the foreground—makes entertaining easy.

SUNSET CONTRIBUTING EDITOR
PETER O. WHITELEY ON

room for dining

❯❯ Seating areas can be intimate, with stationary chairs set close together. For a dining area, more space is needed for comfort and convenience. Allow at least $4\frac{1}{2}$ feet of clearance all around the table. The more room there is, the more gracious the space will feel.

LEFT: A bold, contemporary dining area fits right into a small side yard. The raised terrace is surrounded by steel edging, covered in ¾-inch gold gravel, and furnished with an elegant dining table and benches fashioned from steel and teak.

TOP RIGHT: Tired of that old concrete patio outside the kitchen door? Resurface it with pebbles set in mortar and install garage-sale finds—like mismatched seating, two old side tables joined by a board, and a bright tablecloth—for a chic new look on a budget.

BOTTOM RIGHT: This sunken outdoor dining room features stairs and raised beds made from trimmed granite blocks, an upper patio of decomposed granite, and a lower patio of tightly fitted stone pavers. A portable fire pit and tropical-looking plantings finish the look.

53

outdoor kitchens

TOP LEFT: This grill and oven set is built into a stone counter located away from flammable plants and fences.

TOP RIGHT: Even if your outdoor kitchen is just a portable charcoal grill or a turkey smoker, why not conceal the less-than-lovely appliance inside a stone hutch?

BOTTOM: This all-in-one stone structure includes an expansive countertop with two grills and a sink, space for bar-stool dining, and a stone bench for extra seating "outside" the kitchen.

A comprehensive outdoor kitchen might include cabinets, expansive counters, built-in grill and burners, sink and faucet, refrigerator, and even a wood-burning oven. Take into account the smoke your kitchen will produce and the direction of prevailing winds.

LEFT: Even the simplest open fire is likely to draw people outdoors. This gas-fed fire pit was fashioned from a concrete planter and lightweight stones that conceal the hardware and break up the flames for a natural look.

ABOVE: If you have the space for it—including the large footprint and the vertical space needed for the chimney—a full-sized stone fireplace can make a patio feel like a cozy room.

design lesson

❱❱ Choose a spot for your fire feature that is well away from combustible plants such as ornamental grasses and evergreen trees. Make sure your fire pit is stable and level, and set it up on a hardscape patio, not patio bark. Chimney-top spark arresters and fireplace screens help reduce the hazards of escaping embers.

LEFT: Side-by-side gas fire pits are the focal point of this glamorous garden. Elevated on uneven pedestals, they appear to hover above a bed of decomposed granite. The paving is Marbella limestone, prized for its pale, creamy finish.

TOP RIGHT: This friendly-looking fireplace sits on a gravel patio, accompanied by a traditional arrangement of furniture. The structure was built from concrete blocks and covered with manmade, though convincing, river-rock veneer.

BOTTOM RIGHT: A small, portable fire pit like this can find a home in just about any garden. Easily moved with the changing seasons or for parties, it practically begs for marshmallows to roast.

LEFT: The Arizona flagstone used here for poolside paving is smooth enough for comfortable walking yet rough enough not to be slippery; concrete with exposed aggregate is another popular nonslip option. Along one edge, a series of fountains flow from a low stone wall.

TOP RIGHT: Cut-stone pavers make a graceful walkway around this pool. For the coping, the area directly bordering the pool, a smoother stone was used in consideration of contact with skin and bathing suits.

BOTTOM RIGHT: A multilevel patio links this house and pool, featuring a rough stone wall, smooth coping and paving, and rounded boulders set in and around the pool.

LEFT: Creamy Connecticut bluestone picks up on the hues of the blue-tiled pool and spa for a seamlessly blended patio and pool.

ABOVE: A cut-stone patio extends into a walkway between a swimming pool and pond with fountain. Wide capstones in the foreground provide comfortable seating.

design lesson

›› Transform a plain rectangular pool into something more interesting and natural looking by making one side inaccessible with a low stone wall and planting beds.

LEFT: An elegant semicircular wall separates the gravel patio beneath a sycamore from the wilder garden beyond.

TOP RIGHT: Not every wall has to be perfect. With its top coat of moss and irregular hump, this wall makes no apologies.

BOTTOM RIGHT: In an area where water flows freely, it's important to plan for drainage. This wall has a runnel built in at its base and a drain near its endpoint.

LEFT: The end of a long, zigzagging wall gives privacy to a small pool, complete with a dripping fountain incorporated into the bottom of the wall. A bluestone square offers a lovely spot for sunbathing.

ABOVE: Even though it was built recently, this dry-laid wall has the look of age, thanks to slightly mismatched stones encrusted with lichens and mosses.

design lesson

》 Use walls to define spaces where people can be outdoors but still feel comfortably surrounded. A high wall offers privacy and can help screen noise and create shade. A low wall with a smooth cap can do double duty as a bench.

TOP LEFT: A tasteful mortared structure of Montana wall stone echoes the hues of the gravel patio. Deeply raked joints ensure that the mortar is not visible between stones.

TOP RIGHT: A once-plain concrete-block wall is transformed into something far more elegant with cream-colored veneer, granite capstones, and a built-in bench.

BOTTOM: The homeowners wanted to set off an area of the yard for a new mini-orchard, so they built a low, drystacked wall with an entrance on each side.

This sectioned concrete wall owes its stout appearance to large stones set with wide joints; the stones appear to be reinforcements rather than building blocks.

LEFT: Hefty blocks were used for this handsome dry-stacked retaining wall, which is more than up to the task of holding back the hillside.

TOP RIGHT: Neatly trimmed and casually stacked, these chalky white stones separate lawn from hillside—and they make an attractive raised bed.

BOTTOM RIGHT: When a retaining wall is this high and this close to the house, its construction is a job for professionals. Concrete footings will likely need to be sunk into the soil, drainage will need to be carefully thought out, and a reinforced block wall will need to be in place before the veneer and capstones are added as finishing touches.

LEFT: Contrasting textures give this wall character and style. Wide, smooth, cream-colored capstones stand out above the intricate, multihued face. Even the plantings on the upper level provide interest through variety, with stiffly upright New Zealand flax and billowing yellow coreopsis set against an expanse of lawn.

ABOVE: An undulating retaining wall gradually steps down a gentle slope. The planting near the wall's edge provides particularly fast drainage, which is exactly what succulents like hen-and-chicks need to thrive.

design lesson

❯❯ A long, high retaining wall can look industrial and stark. To soften the look and break up the massive face of a wall, plant cascading vines or billowing perennials above the wall, or plant a tree in front of it.

gabion
walls

LEFT: A gabion is simply a wire cage filled with rocks. The resulting structure is strong enough to use as a retaining wall—and bold enough to stand out as an industrial-chic design statement.

ABOVE: Simple, modern, and elegant, this tall gabion wall comprises a small-mesh cage filled with small stones. Metal beams and evenly spaced bolts provide additional strength, and the top is left unfilled to draw attention to how the wall works.

SUNSET CONTRIBUTING EDITOR
PETER O. WHITELEY ON

recycling

» Gabion walls present a great opportunity for using recycled materials like broken bricks, repurposed gravel, or random mixes of leftover stone from other projects. As long as the diameter of each piece is larger than the openings of the wire mesh, you can choose any material you like to create your gabion wall.

LEFT: Measuring just 8 by 12 feet, this raised bed was built with stacked flagstones left over from construction of the adjacent patio. Three glazed pots in lime green catch the eye and add color.

TOP RIGHT: This U-shaped raised planter, fashioned from concrete block with limestone veneer, offers easy access to edible crops.

BOTTOM RIGHT: Situated at right angles to a wood panel wall and matching bench, this low wall of pale stones forms a raised bed that's as artistic as it is functional.

TOP LEFT: A casually stacked raised bed along the sidewalk showcases variegated hostas in full bloom and gives a cottagey flavor to the front yard.

TOP RIGHT: Blue fescue contrasts beautifully with a white stucco raised bed built alongside steps. The reflected heat benefits the grasses, especially in cool-summer areas.

BOTTOM: This creative garden feature is part swirling path, part raised bed. Small river boulders in a variety of colors and shapes were used to build the casual walls.

Stepping down a sloping front yard, these terraced beds make a gracious yet casual entry to a Santa Fe home. Note how the stones' orange and pink tones match those of the house and arbor.

boulders

LEFT: A well-placed group of boulders works beautifully to mark a transition in the garden. Surrounded by various ornamental grasses and illuminated at night, these large stones signal the shift from patio to path, with a set of wooden steps that tempt you to sit for a closer look at the stony surfaces.

ABOVE: Boulders usually look best when placed as they might appear in a natural landscape. There you will usually find them partially buried rather than sitting fully on top of the ground. This group—woven together with a low-growing ground cover—looks like a natural outcropping and makes a subtle but powerful focal point in a lawn.

SUNSET GARDEN EDITOR KATHLEEN NORRIS BRENZEL ON

boulder placement

》 Boulders are powerful design elements. You might think that randomly scattering them would create a natural look, but this rarely works. To make a graceful composition around a large rounded boulder, choose a smaller reclining rock and a low, flat rock—all of their shapes look relaxed.

LEFT: Even a few small boulders placed next to a path can make a striking design statement. These three—chosen to match the fountain basin nearby—were stood on end like three sentinels in a bed of baby's tears and white impatiens.

TOP RIGHT: What could be more dramatic than a group of huge stones arranged as if they had tumbled down from the mountainside and stopped just short of the front door?

BOTTOM RIGHT: If you're lucky enough to have boulders like these on your site, work your design around them. Between the stones, tuck in rugged plants like burgundy New Zealand flax, soft gray artemisia, and blue oat grass.

83

stone accents & garden art

TOP LEFT: When they demolished an old sidewalk and patio, the homeowners made good use of the broken concrete by building steps and a small raised bed that juts into the lawn. A granite globe was an inspired finishing touch.

BOTTOM LEFT: You can use stone to make almost any kind of accent, even a kitchen sink. Set into a custom-carved wooden countertop, this rustic basin catches hot and cold running water.

RIGHT: Partially hidden in a far corner of the garden, this venerable millstone beckons observers to journey up the plant-packed stairs. A bold piece like this could be equally effective standing alone in the center of a modern courtyard.

LEFT: A low mortared wall is the perfect place to highlight an eclectic assortment of large and small river stones, flagstone remnants, and assorted carved pieces. Medium-sized pebbles piled against the base give the impression that the wall is flowing into the path.

ABOVE: Blurring the boundaries between home and garden, this stone slab seems to pass through a window to hang over a pool. The illusion was created with two stones with cleanly sliced ends, one placed inside and one out.

design lesson

>> When choosing stone pieces for use in the garden, don't worry about flaws like chipped edges or stained surfaces. The more weathered a piece looks, the more interest it holds in the landscape.

TOP LEFT: This original piece of stone art was made from a river-tumbled cobble wrapped in a steel rod.

TOP RIGHT: Anything goes when you're combining outdoor stone accents. A whimsical three-pawed table, a cushioned bench, and a realistically carved ornament make this a fun corner of the garden.

BOTTOM: A rough-hewn table comes in handy as a stand for plants and decorative pieces. It also works well as a buffet when there's a party in the garden.

This graceful ornament is a stylized take on a traditional lantern style based on ancient Japanese cosmology. The piece incorporates five parts, symbolizing the five elements (from the top down): sky, wind, fire, water, and earth.

stone benches

With thick cushions and assorted pillows, this bench is almost as comfortable and stylish as an indoor sofa—complete with a stone "coffee table."

TOP LEFT: A simple and appealing bench makes a bold horizontal line against a stucco wall.

TOP RIGHT: Smooth, light-colored stones were mortared together to form this shady resting spot. The stones stay cool in the tree's shade.

BOTTOM: Chunky and primitive, this piece is as much garden art as it is garden furniture.

rock
gardens

LEFT: Traditional rock gardens of dwarf conifers and diminutive alpine plants are not often seen these days, but you can create a casual rock garden wherever small plants can be tucked in around stones. Fill crevices in a rocky stairway with plants that thrive on good drainage and the reflected heat of the stone. Or make a slab garden by having a boulder broken into pieces at the stone yard and reassembling it in the garden, leaving gaps for gravel, soil, and appropriate small plants.

ABOVE: A gentle slope is the perfect spot for a casual rockery. A few good-sized boulders were secured on the hillside, and more were grouped in an informal line along the bottom to retain the slope. For any type of rock garden, a good formula is two-fifths rock and three-fifths plants.

design lesson

❯❯ Make a rock outcropping on a flat site by mounding soil into a berm and placing jagged rocks onto the face of it so that they seem to have been forced upward out of the bedrock.

gravel gardens

TOP LEFT: A courtyard in the Mediterranean style is a natural spot for a gravel garden planted with lavender, New Zealand flax, and olive trees.

TOP RIGHT: Light gray gravel is the perfect foil for colorful, drought-tolerant plants.

BOTTOM: Create a Japanese-style gravel garden with a few boulders in a sea of sharp-edged gravel. To suggest waves or create abstract patterns, rake the gravel with a garden fork or an old rake with every other tine removed.

Replace a boring lawn with golden gravel dotted with an ornamental grass like deer grass (*Muhlenbergia rigens*), then add a few accent plants like blue-leaved Weber agave.

LEFT: Steel-blue century plant (*Agave americana*), yellow-flowered mesquite (*Prosopis*), and gray-stemmed ocotillo (*Fouquieria splendens*) are like sculptures when arranged against a blood-red wall.

ABOVE: Use edging to separate different shades of gravel, and you can create any pattern you like. This Phoenix gravel patio features desert trees for shade and a cooling water feature next to the house.

design lesson

>> If you're looking for a way to save water, transform part or all of your lawn into a gravel garden filled with drought-tolerant plants. Many unthirsty plants share the need for excellent drainage, which gravel provides. Gravel also reflects heat, which is a plus for many of these plants when they are grown in cooler climes.

LEFT: Recirculating spill fountains—like this one burbling next to a flagstone path— appear to be perpetually overflowing. Water flows down the sides into a buried catch basin that houses the fountain's pump.

TOP RIGHT: Concrete pavers surround an impressive 7-foot concrete fountain on a bed of gravel. Attached to a simple copper pipe is a fountainhead, which can be changed to alter the spray pattern from a bubbler to a soft spray to a vertical jet.

BOTTOM RIGHT: This fern-dotted wall fountain pours water down its stony surface into a rectangular catch basin. The effect is visually—and physically—cooling.

TOP LEFT: A boar's-head fountain makes a glittering splash in a stone pool.

TOP RIGHT: This classic urn fountain keeps the water moving in the goldfish pond, thereby reducing the likelihood of breeding mosquitoes.

BOTTOM: An edgy, industrial-looking urn is just the thing for this minimalist flagstone patio. If you place your fountain where people can touch it, they won't be able to resist.

In a dry landscape, a water feature is especially effective. This pondless fountain cools the air around it and makes a refreshing focal point.

LEFT: A reflecting pool brings a strip of sky down into the garden. With colorful, varied plantings all around, this garden benefits from the serene composition, made even more placid by the choice of smooth, neutral-hued pavers along the pool's edges.

ABOVE: With two waterfalls—one tumbling down a rocky bank and the other streaming from an urn—this pond fills the backyard with the sound of water. Broad flagstones near the water's edge invite closer inspection. If young children will be visiting your garden, be sure to restrict access to any pond or pool area with fencing and a locking gate.

design lesson

>> Here's a straightforward way to add a raised pond to a small garden space: Build stone walls to contain a pond liner, then add stone coping to conceal the works.

TOP LEFT: To create the illusion of an infinity pool, water has to drop over an edge that is not visible from the surface. Here, that overflow goes into an attractive collecting pool.

TOP RIGHT: The upper pond is planted, while the lower one simply recirculates water through a large copper dish shaped to form three streams.

BOTTOM: A bluestone walkway takes you through a shallow pool planted with water lilies and punctuated by a dramatic bluestone boulder.

From its seat-wall reservoir, water slips down a green limestone spillway and into a pool. The smooth concrete of the reservoir contrasts subtly with the exposed-aggregate patio, and the boulders add their own peaceful distinction to the scene.

water
bowls

LEFT: If a fountain or pond doesn't seem right for your garden but you still want a water feature, consider a simple water bowl. You can get that lovely "mirror to the sky" effect by keeping the bowl full to the brim. Some boulders—like these sections of basalt—have natural depressions that will hold water. Add pebbles to act as landing pads for butterflies and dragonflies.

TOP RIGHT: Even a diminutive carved-stone bowl can catch rainwater or stay filled by irrigation sprinklers. This bright little bowl gets frequent use as a birdbath.

BOTTOM RIGHT: To suggest a natural seep, place your water bowl near the bottom of a slope, and plant grasses nearby.

outdoor showers

In this Phoenix garden, a refreshing stream drops from a stylish copper canopy.

Provided you live in the right climate, an outdoor shower can be an exciting and useful addition to your garden. With just a bit of privacy screening and access to a hot-water line, you're ready to get wet. Interlocking tiles set with pebbles create a pleasing backsplash for this outdoor shower in Los Angeles.

The owners of this San Diego beach house wanted a place to rinse off after surfing, so they installed a shower with a slate back-splash and a faux-stone sidewall next to the rear stairs.

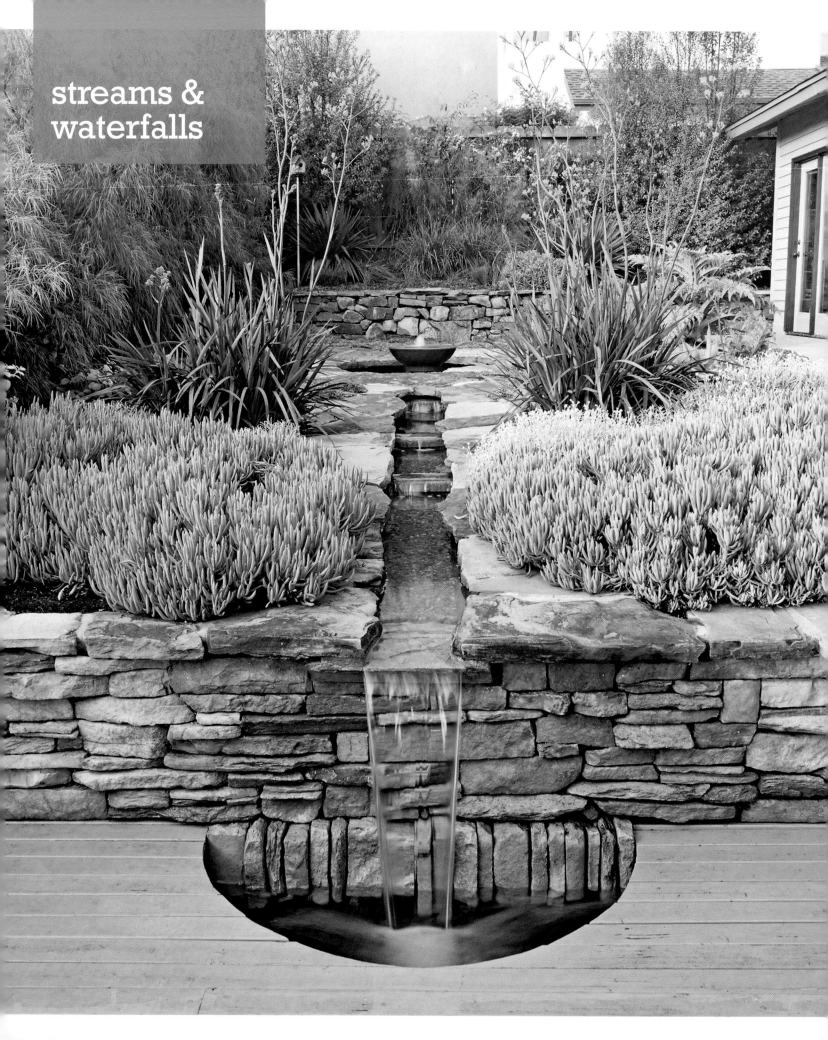

LEFT: Connecting the upper and lower pools of this imaginative water feature is a rill constructed from stacked flagstones. Water runs over a series of small falls stepping down the slope and into a collecting basin concealed beneath a deck.

RIGHT: A naturalistic stream with falls incorporates rounded boulders and flat ledge stones with a planted pond at the bottom. Stones of various sizes line the pond, making this water feature seem even more realistic.

FAR RIGHT: Chunky blocks lead the water to a long, unbroken fall in this modern take on a stream and waterfall.

SUNSET GARDEN EDITOR
KATHLEEN NORRIS BRENZEL ON

water sounds

》 Think carefully about the sound you want your water feature to make. If the water moves too slowly or smoothly, you may not hear much at all. If it gushes loudly, it can be distracting to you or your neighbors. You may wish to install an adjustable pump to make water move at different speeds.

LEFT: A thoughtfully sited dry creek bed simulates the course water would take if it were present, following the path of least resistance as it slips downhill and curves around the slightest rise. This natural-looking example is edged with ornamental grasses and orange-flowered torch lily.

TOP RIGHT: A massive boulder gives this dry creek bed a reason to curve, and it's a great sitting place as well.

BOTTOM RIGHT: To break up a long stretch, use flagstones to build a "bridge" across the dry creek bed. River pebbles are a natural choice, since they were shaped by water-driven tumbling.

LEFT: In a desert landscape, even the suggestion of water has a powerful impact. Here, larger rough stones give way to smaller rounded ones, and a gravel wash is simulated at the lowest level.

ABOVE: In a shady woodland setting, a natural-looking creek bed might be surrounded by ferns and lush shrubbery. If your property has a drainage problem, an open streambed such as this one could be a less expensive alternative to an underground French drain.

design lesson

›› Even though water may only rarely flow through your creek bed, design it with water in mind. Take the dry stream around a promontory and past a beach downstream, and place a stepping-stone midstream to create the illusion of leaving shore.

How to Build

There's something deeply satisfying about working with stone, partly because it's such an ancient activity and partly because the material itself is already eons old. Durable and timeless, stone is a fine choice for just about any landscape feature, from rugged, naturalistic paths to modern, formal-looking fountains and precisely laid patios. Building with stone is slow, patient work—a welcome relief from a fast-paced world where it's not always easy to see the fruits of your labor. The work is rewarding because of the natural beauty of the result and the feeling that you have created something permanent. In this chapter, you'll find basic instructions for a wide range of projects, as well as tips on design, construction, and safety from *Sunset's* experts. Gather your tools, plan your project, and join the long tradition of landscaping with stone.

Even sophisticated stonescapes like this one are feasible when broken down into smaller projects. A retaining wall holds back the hill and is in turn partially supported by stone steps. On the lower level, boulders surround a cut-stone patio and a distinctive fountain nestled in a bed of pebbles.

evaluating the site

Careful checking ensured that this new path would not interfere with buried lines and that the wall would be low enough not to require a permit.

Before you begin any landscaping project, such as installing a stone patio, a path, or a wall, assess the area on which you plan to build for a variety of factors that could have a major impact on how you approach your project. A slight change in your design, such as curving a path slightly to avoid a buried obstacle, can make your project much easier.

TAKING STOCK Plan ahead for a smooth project.

» **Locate** property lines to be sure your project doesn't cross into a neighbor's yard.

» **Check** with your local municipality regarding zoning restrictions, setbacks, rights-of-way, and permit requirements.

» **Check** with your utility company for the location of buried water, gas, sewer, or electric lines.

» **Identify** soil type. If your soil is light and sandy, water will drain away faster, and it will be easier to adjust the position of stones set in soil. Heavy clay soil drains more slowly and can dry to fix stones firmly in place.

» **Note** the topography. Slopes drain more quickly, and water may pool in low spots. A stone path leading uphill may need steps, or you might be able to curve the path around the rise so that steps are not needed. A steep slope might be broken up with a retaining wall that divides it into terraces.

» **Notice** the pattern of sun and shade. A patio might be sited where it's warmed by the morning sun but pleasantly shady during hot afternoons.

» **Identify** plants you want to keep; they may need protection during construction. If a tree or shrub is going to be removed, it's best to do it early in the process so you can get a feeling for the space without it.

» **Plan** for access. Large projects may require a clear route to the street for deliveries of stone or a spot for unloading soil.

» **Think** about where you might be able to use any excess soil if you'll be excavating. When digging a foundation for a path, for instance, consider building low mounds on either side.

» **Draw** a plan of how your project will fit into the existing landscape. This can be a simple sketch or a more detailed plan drawn to scale.

SUNSET HEAD GARDENER
RICK LAFRENTZ ON

budgeting

A variety of factors may affect the budget for your project, among them the cost of permits, charges for the removal of existing landscaping materials, equipment rentals, tool purchases, and contractor fees. Do your best, however, to estimate the cost of your building materials. Boulders and stone for walls are priced by weight; base rock, sand, and gravel are sold by the cubic yard; and flagstone and cut stone are sold by the square foot. Visit a local stone yard to get an idea of the costs for various types of stone. Local stone is usually cheaper. Remember to ask too about delivery charges.

providing for drainage

Whenever you pave an area, its drainage is affected, because water tends to run off even the most porous of paving materials. The natural drainage of the site is also affected when you put a large solid object, such as a concrete retaining wall or a pond, in the soil.

Unless the site slopes naturally, grade before you pave so that runoff won't collect where it can cause problems—against a house foundation, for example. Allow a pitch of at least 1 inch per 8 feet (or 1/8 inch per foot). Pay particular attention to grading any large areas of impermeable paving; gravel paths on a bed of sand probably won't need as much attention. Even large boulders can cause the soil to sink around them, creating a low spot where water will pool.

DRAIN CONSTRUCTION Keep your path or patio puddle-free.

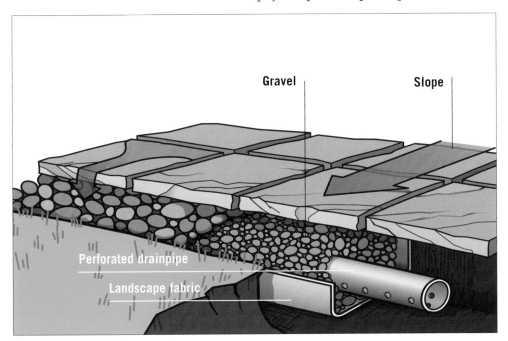

Gravel

Slope

Perforated drainpipe

Landscape fabric

If you are planning a large patio or have soil that drains poorly, you may need to provide an easy way for water to flow safely away. Dig a trench about 12 inches deep (deeper in areas where the ground freezes) on the downward edge of the patio and line it with filter cloth. Then add perforated pipe, with the holes pointed down so gravel won't plug them. If your property slopes, extend the trench and add unperforated pipe to carry the water

downhill to a point where it can flow out and not be a problem. If your land is flat, extend the pipe instead to a gravel-filled pit away from all structures.

Before you cover up the pipe, check with a level to make sure all sections slant downhill. Then cover the pipe loosely with additional filter cloth and fill around the perforated sections with round, washed gravel. Cover solid sections of pipe with soil.

design lesson

›› Permeable paving lets rainwater drain into a deep gravel layer underneath. It's good for the environment because the water slowly percolates through the paving into the soil, reducing storm-water runoff that tends to carry pollutants into local water supplies. Another benefit: no puddles on top of your path or patio during the rainy season.

excavating

Extensive excavation was needed for this generously proportioned patio, which includes a recirculating fountain. The leftover soil was used to fill raised beds around the edges.

Many stone projects require excavations for foundation and drainage materials. A simple way to excavate to the correct depth across a wide area is to lay out twine between stakes and take your measurements from the twine as you dig. Any adjustments for grading can be incorporated. The directions that follow are for patios, but they'll work for any project.

laying foundations

» No matter what type of stone paving you choose, you will probably have to prepare a foundation, or subbase. Although it's heavy work pouring gravel and sand or concrete, don't skimp on the construction, or the paving may buckle and sink. For large areas, equip yourself with back-saving tools—a sturdy wheelbarrow is a must. Or consider having a contractor lay the foundation materials for you. The foundation needs to be particularly deep if your soil is unstable—if it floods, for example, or heaves from frost. As you plan your project, bear in mind that small, thin paving units are more likely to be sent askew by movement in the soil than large, thick slabs of stone.

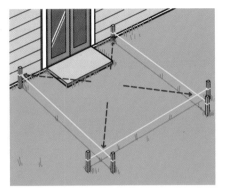

❶ Stake the Perimeter

Use stakes and string to mark the area you need to excavate. Keep the stakes back a bit, as shown, so they aren't in your way as you dig and build the patio. To be sure the corners are all right angles, measure the distance between each stake next to the house and the corner diagonally across from it. The two distances should be equal.

❷ Mark the Height

Mark the eventual height of the patio on the stakes, being sure to measure up far enough to clear lawn or other vegetation. You can do this by marking the patio height on one stake next to the house and tying a string to that spot. Then stretch the string to the stake straight out from the house and tie a knot. Slip on a line level (a small tool that hooks over the string) and raise or lower the second knot until the string is level. Mark that height and repeat the process until you have marked all stakes.

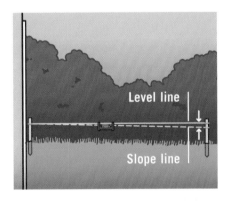

Level line

Slope line

❸ Set the Slope

Divide the distance the patio extends out from the house, in feet, by 8. The result is the number of inches the patio must slope away from the house to ensure that rainwater will drain. On the outer stakes, measure down by this amount from the first marks you made. This is the finished elevation, plus the gap you left to clear vegetation.

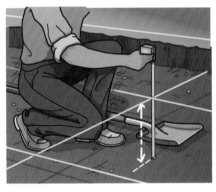

❹ Excavate

Using these reference points, excavate soil, add base materials, and install edging, as you would for a path. If it's a large area, you might need additional reference lines. Just add more stakes and string every 5 feet or so.

working safely

Wear eye protection when chipping or cutting stone. Protect your ears with earmuffs or plugs when operating power tools, and don a mask before working with materials that throw off dust.

Working with stone is rewarding but heavy work. Take precautions to avoid injury. Wear sturdy boots and gloves when you're transporting heavy materials, and keep out of the way of a stone that might roll or a wheelbarrow that might tip. On slopes, always start work from the base and embed each stone firmly before bringing the next piece into place. Don't bite off more than you can chew. Start out with the right equipment for the work and, if necessary, make it a team project, enlisting the help of friends.

It's also important to build well, so that the finished project doesn't pose a safety hazard. Consult your local building department about codes as necessary. Hire a landscape architect or an engineer if your site has drainage or erosion problems or if you're building on a steep slope or on fill. As you plan, imagine the finished project: Will children rush to the water's edge? Will the path be used after dark? Are the steps comfortable for people of all ages? Be smart and figure all these things out before you begin.

MOVING HEAVY STONES   Get the job done without injuries.

Lift with Your Legs

Avoid lifting heavy stones into position whenever possible so you don't hurt your back. Drag, roll, tip, or pry them instead. When you absolutely must lift, squat down and grab hold of the stone; then, keeping your back straight and the stone close to your body, lift with your legs. A lifting belt can help prevent strain.

Use a Ramp

To raise a large stone into position without actually picking it up, make a simple 2 x 12 ramp with 2 x 2 crosspieces screwed to it every 16 inches or so. Carefully roll the stone up the ramp. The crosspieces will keep the stones from sliding back.

Use a Hand Truck

To transport boulders, large stones, or heavy bags, a hand truck is highly recommended. A model with air-filled tires is easiest to push and less likely to damage a lawn. Work with a helper to load the stone, then tilt the hand truck back until you feel no pressure on the handle.

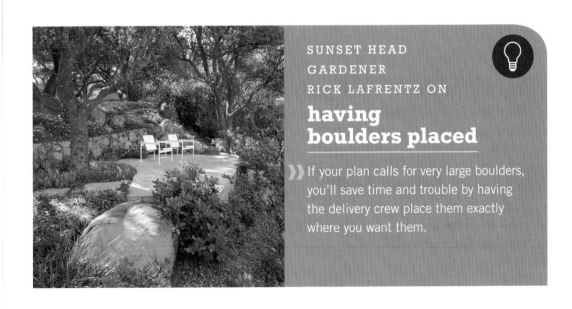

SUNSET HEAD
GARDENER
RICK LAFRENTZ ON

having boulders placed

If your plan calls for very large boulders, you'll save time and trouble by having the delivery crew place them exactly where you want them.

stepping-stone paths

Large stepping-stones laid on a sand base require little digging and can be moved easily if you change your mind about the path's direction.

Stepping-stones are fun and easy to lay. Arrange them differently in different areas of the garden—spaced generously (10 to 12 inches apart) to quicken people's pace through a storage area or close together (4 to 6 inches) to slow people down to admire the flowers. The larger the gaps, the larger the stones should be in order to look good and provide sure footing. If you are building a path for a slower pace, you can use smaller stones, but don't choose pieces less than 18 inches long or the path will seem less gracious and inviting. Be sure your stones are of roughly uniform thickness.

Set stepping-stones in soil so that the tops are 1 or 2 inches above ground; this will help keep mud off the path. If you want to surround the stones with pebbles or new plants, you will need to clear the entire area first. However, avoid digging too deep, because you'll need to replace any disturbed soil under the stones with gravel or sand. Stepping-stone paths across a lawn are often laid flush with the soil so that a mower can run right over the stones.

❶ Plan the Route

Lay out the stepping-stones in a pleasing line, arranged so the spaces between them provide a comfortable, regular pace. Place them along the route so that their longest dimension runs across the path, not in line with it.

❷ Mark Positions

Cut around each stone with a spade or a knife to mark its shape, then tip the stone on an edge and roll it to one side. Make note of its orientation so you can reposition it exactly when the time comes.

❸ Excavate Cut a hole

for the stone with a straight-edged spade. Slice the edges straight down, then remove soil or turf within the outline. For a path laid in soil, make the hole half as deep as the thickness of the stone plus 1 inch; this will allow for sand beneath the stones.

❹ Lay a Sand Base

Spread 1 inch of sand in the hole, and wet it with a fine spray of water. Tip the stone back into place in the hole and twist it into the sand until the stone is level and firm.

❺ Fill the Edges Add

more sand around the stone and pack the edges. Water with a fine spray to settle the sand. Repeat these steps for the remaining stones.

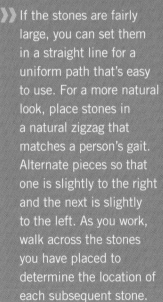

design lesson

❯❯ If the stones are fairly large, you can set them in a straight line for a uniform path that's easy to use. For a more natural look, place stones in a natural zigzag that matches a person's gait. Alternate pieces so that one is slightly to the right and the next is slightly to the left. As you work, walk across the stones you have placed to determine the location of each subsequent stone.

path & patio edgings

Concrete pavers marching through a metal-edged bed of stone chips make for a simple, contemporary path.

Gravel paths require edging material, and most other stone pathways benefit from it as well. Besides helping to lock the paving into place, edging material often contributes significantly to the overall appeal of a path. Some edging is barely notice-able—a good choice if you want to create an illusion that your path is winding naturally across a site. The types of edging described on the facing page will work with a variety of paving materials and can be used for patios as well.

Cut Stone Edging

Cut stone set on edge creates an especially elegant look. Set the top edge so it will extend 1 or 1½ inches above the gravel or other paving material. Butt the edging pieces tightly. If you are using mortar between joints on the path, use it between edging pieces as well.

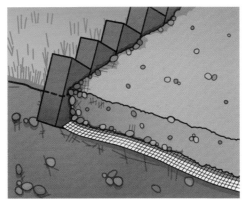

Brick Edging

Bricks provide a traditional touch that's equally at home in a formal garden or one with a cottage feel. Stand bricks on end, "soldier" style, or place pieces at a 45-degree angle.

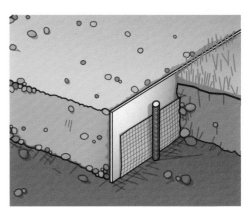

Metal Edging

Metal is tidy and unobtrusive. Use metal strips fabricated as edging. Or buy ⅛-inch-by-4-inch flat stock (used by blacksmiths) from an iron supply company and pin it in place with rebar about 12 inches long.

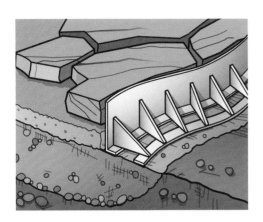

Plastic Edging

Plastic edging is available at masonry-supply stores in several styles. For gravel paths, get rolls with a wide, rounded top edge. For stone paving at least 1½ inches thick, look for the type designed for brick paving (shown in the illustration).

Wood Edging

Wood or composites of plastic and wood fiber also make attractive edging. Wood should be either naturally rot-resistant (such as the dark-colored heartwood of cedar or redwood) or pressure-treated with preservatives. For curves, use benderboard, which is about ⅜ inch thick, or a flexible type of composite lumber.

design lesson

▶▶ Edging can make a strong statement as part of a path design. You can choose a color or texture that contrasts with the paving material—or call attention to the edging by making it a little taller or wider than absolutely necessary.

gravel paths & patios

This pretty little path follows a graceful curve to a circular patio—and the whole project is easily finished in just a weekend.

Gravel—either smooth river rock that rolls underfoot or more stable, mechanically crushed rock—makes a low-cost, fast-draining path or patio surface that can look great in many different styles of gardens. It's easy to install and easy to remove in case you make a change to your garden design.

❶ Cut Your Route

Mark the outline of your path, then excavate 6 to 8 inches down. Cut deeply enough along the edges of the path bed to allow the edging materials to be 1 to 1½ inches higher than the surrounding soil. If your path crosses a lawn, remove the sod with roots intact so it can be used elsewhere.

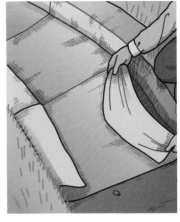

❷ Line the Bed Install

landscape fabric, if you are using it. Cut it wide enough to extend under the edging and perhaps even wrap up the outside almost to the soil line. Overlap pieces by 12 to 18 inches.

❸ Build an Edge

Install whatever edging you have chosen. See pages 130–131 for more about edgings. If you've used landscape fabric, be careful not to tear it.

❹ Prepare a Base

Add a 3-inch base of crushed gravel. If the path area has poor drainage, use pieces with a diameter of ¾ inch; if drainage is good, the gravel size isn't critical.

❺ Add Next Layer

Rake the gravel into a uniform layer, then dampen it. Use a fine spray of water to nudge tiny pieces of gravel into crevices between larger particles.

❻ Complete the

Path After any standing water has disappeared, pass over the area several times with a hand tamper to pack the gravel firmly. Add the remaining gravel, working in no more than 3-inch layers; dampen and tamp each layer. You can skip the tamping on the final layer.

cut stone
on sand

Tightly fitted stone pavers make a smooth, uniform surface for a patio.

Cut stone laid on a bed of sand makes a surprisingly sturdy path or patio, provided the edgings are strong, the stone is laid in a tight pattern, and the joints are kept tightly packed with sand. Sand-bedding the stones provides a flexible surface that allows for easy repair should tree roots or frosts cause the underlying surface to buckle. Also, if a stone is damaged, it can be replaced easily if it has been laid in sand.

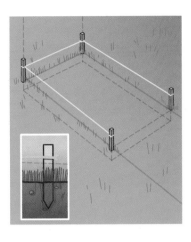

❶ Mark Your Site

Lay out the perimeter using stakes and string. When the stakes are in place, mark one at the eventual height of the paving, then measure up by a distance that clears the grass or other landscaping. Make another mark there. With string and a line level, transfer this height to the other stakes. For drainage, allow for a slope of ⅛ to ¼ inch per foot.

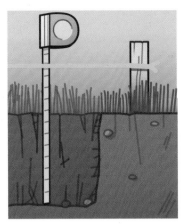

❷ Excavate
Dig a hole at least 7 inches deep where winters are mild or 12 inches where the ground freezes. If you are not using edging or are using a deep type, such as cut stone set vertically, excavate just to the edge of the path. If you are using metal or plastic edging pinned with stakes, go out 8 inches beyond the path's perimeter.

❸ Build a Base
Install the gravel base and add edging, if you are using it, when the gravel is at the appropriate height. If you will not be using an edging, install temporary 2 x 4 edge forms to contain the gravel. Add the gravel in increments 3 inches deep, dampening the gravel and compacting, before adding another layer. Build up the gravel until there's just enough room for the sand and stones.

❹ Top with Sand

Add the sand and roughly level it with a rake. Tamp. Take out high spots and find low spots to fill by running a screed along the edging or temporary edge forms. When the sand is level, compact it a final time and saturate it with a fine mist of water. Wait overnight for it to drain completely. Run the screed along the path a final time and level any uneven spots.

❺ Install the Stone

Aim to create equally sized joints, usually about ½ inch wide, but don't worry if you need to fudge by ⅛ inch or so to accommodate differences in the stones. Use a mallet to seat each stone, then check its alignment with a level. If you need to move a stone, avoid creating ruts in the base.

❻ Fill the Gaps
After you have set all the full stones, cut and install the partial pieces. Fill the joints with sand. Do this by tossing the sand over the stones and sweeping it into the joints. Spray the path lightly with water and repeat until no more sand goes into the joints.

flagstone on sand

A casual circular patio surrounded by fast-growing grasses and ground covers can transform a plain corner of the backyard into a garden getaway. Just add comfortable chairs.

Here's an easy weekend project: installing an 8-foot-wide circular flagstone patio on a sand base. Buy about ¾ ton of flagstone pieces. Shop for flagstones that are 1 to 2 inches thick and 1 to 3 feet long, and choose as many straight-sided pieces as possible.

If your site is poorly drained or you live in an area where the ground freezes, make your excavation 6 inches deeper and add a base layer of gravel topped with landscape fabric.

❶ Define the Area Choose a level site and rake the area smooth, then mark the perimeter by tracing around a center stake with a stick tied to a 4-foot-long. string. Mark this outline with a garden hose, then remove soil to a depth of 3 inches. Check for level with a long 2 x 4 taped to a level. Fill the circle with 2 to 3 inches of sand, raked smooth, moistened, tamped, and checked again for level.

❷ Place the Stones Starting at the outer edge, position the large stones to sit slightly above the surrounding soil surface. Arrange them as carefully as possible for fit. Place as many large pieces as possible, then fill in with smaller pieces. Check the level of the patio regularly.

❸ Cut Stones Wearing goggles, use a chisel and mallet to break stones into smaller pieces. Place a stone atop a board, scrape a line on the stone where you want to make a cut, then gently strike the chisel there to make a ⅛-inch-deep depression. Finally, pound the stone hard until it breaks.

❹ Fill in the Cracks Remove the hose. Shovel sand over the patio surface and sweep it into cracks. Spray the sand with water to make it settle, then apply more sand and sweep again to fill the cracks.

flagstone in mortar

Elegant sand-colored flagstone with smoothly mortared joints creates a stylish patio floor that looks finished enough to be indoors.

An old concrete patio makes a good base for mortared flagstone, presuming the concrete is clean and in good condition. If you pour a new slab, rough up the hardening concrete with a broom so the mortar will adhere. Let the concrete cure for at least three days before you begin the stonework. If you are using edging, install it before fitting the flagstones, resting the edging on the concrete, if possible.

Trial-fit and trim all the flagstones. If the underlying concrete includes relief joints, keep stones to either side of them to prevent cracks. When all the stones are in place, remove pieces in a section of about 10 or 12 square feet and set them, in order, to the side. Dampen the concrete and the stones, and blot up any standing water. Prepare a bagged mortar mix or a homemade batch of 1 part masonry cement to 3 parts sand, plus just enough water to make a stiff mixture.

SETTING FLAGSTONES Create firm paving with uniform joints.

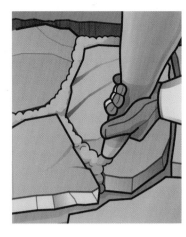
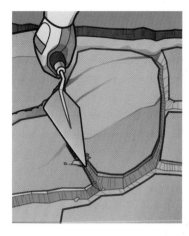

❶ Lay the Mortar

With a pointed trowel, spread mortar over an area big enough for at least two stones. Make a layer 1 inch thick, or even thicker if the stone for that spot is unusually thin. Think of the mortar as a leveling device. Furrow the mortar with the trowel.

❷ Set the Stone

Lower a stone onto the mortar and embed it by tapping with a rubber mallet. Don't force the mortar to gush up around the stone, however. Set subsequent stones in the same way. As you proceed, check the surface with a level to make sure that it slopes at least ⅛ inch per foot. Clean the stones with a damp sponge as you go.

❸ Grout the Joints

Let the mortar set 24 hours, then grout the joints with a fresh batch of mortar. Apply it with a mortar bag, which is like an oversize cake-decorating bag, or with a trowel. Aim to make the mortar flush with the surface of the stone. Do not attempt to smooth the mortar immediately or you'll make a mess.

❹ Shape the Grout

Shape the mortar when it stiffens a bit. With your trowel, press down on the grout to force it into any hidden crevices. Then shape the top surface as you wish—you can smooth it flat or push it down to make V-shaped valleys. Or use a wire loop to cut a slightly rounded indentation. Cut off excess grout and remove it. Keep it damp for at least three days by misting the patio with water and covering it with plastic.

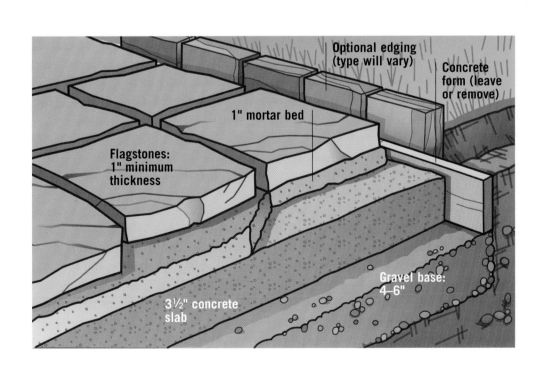

Optional edging (type will vary)

Concrete form (leave or remove)

1" mortar bed

Flagstones: 1" minimum thickness

3½" concrete slab

Gravel base: 4–6"

pebble
mosaics

Once you have mastered the basic technique, you can let your imagination be your guide for fanciful pebble mosaics such as this circular path.

Pebble mosaics are fun to make, but they're more time-consuming than you might expect. You might want to limit your first project to no more than 2 or 3 feet square.

Draw a full-size pattern and gather enough stones to carry it out. Stones must be placed with their longest dimension upright, so you will use many more pieces than you might anticipate. As a setting medium in which to install your pebbles, use a mixture of 1 part portland cement, 2 parts 1/4-inch crushed gravel (with or without smaller particles), and 3 parts sand. You will use a slightly different mixture once the pebbles are installed. Depending on the type of edging you choose (see pages 130–131), install it either before or after you have laid in the full gravel base.

❶ Prepare the Bed
Mark the perimeter, then excavate to a depth of 7 inches where winters are mild or 12 inches where soil freezes. Install your edging. Using 5/8-inch crushed gravel with finer particles included, spread a 3-inch base, spray it with water, then tamp the gravel down with a hand tamper. Repeat until there is enough space between the gravel and the top of the edging for the longest stones to stand upright with at least 1/2 inch to spare.

❷ Subdivide If you are attempting a large mosaic, install dividers so that you work in areas no larger than you can complete in a day. From 1/4-inch plywood, cut out patterns that match key elements of your design. You can set stones freehand, but patterns will speed the work and produce better results. Fill all but the top 3/4 inch within the form with the setting mixture.

❸ Place Stones Set the patterns onto the sand-cement mixture. Starting next to the patterns, embed pebbles partway into the setting mixture. Pieces must touch each other and must have their longest dimension vertical. When you wedge the final piece into place, the stones will become more stable.

❹ Finish a Section
Remove the patterns and fill in the remaining areas. Then place a straight board across the form and tap it down to seat the stones evenly. Repeat this across the entire mosaic (or the area you are completing that day).

❺ Fill the Joints
Wearing a dust mask, thoroughly mix 1 part portland cement and 3 parts fine sand (or use a bagged sand-cement mixture). Sprinkle the mixture over the mosaic and brush it into all crevices.

❻ Wet the Surface
Mist with water. Use a garden sprayer rather than a hose so you don't create puddles or wash away the sand. If holes appear, add more of the sand-cement mixture and mist again. Cover the area with plastic and anchor all edges with wood or stones. Spray periodically, keeping the area damp, for at least 4 days; up to 24 days is ideal.

simple stone steps

Don't underestimate the sheer mass of large slabs of stone; you'll need either a heavy piece of equipment or three strong-backed friends to help you move even the modest-sized slabs shown here.

If you need just a few steps and have a way to move heavy slabs to the site, you can build a stepping-stone staircase. Well-designed steps have good proportions. The flat part of the step, called the tread, is nicely in proportion to the vertical element, the riser. This formula sums up what works: The depth of the treads plus twice the rise should equal 25 to 27 inches. For this project, choose stones about 24 inches wide, 16 inches long, and 6 inches thick. These dimensions will provide 6-inch risers, 16-by-24-inch treads, and 1 inch of overlap.

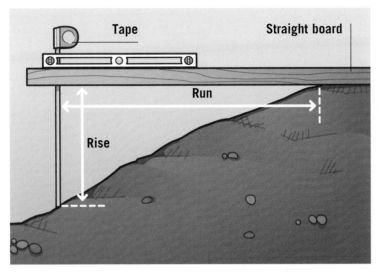

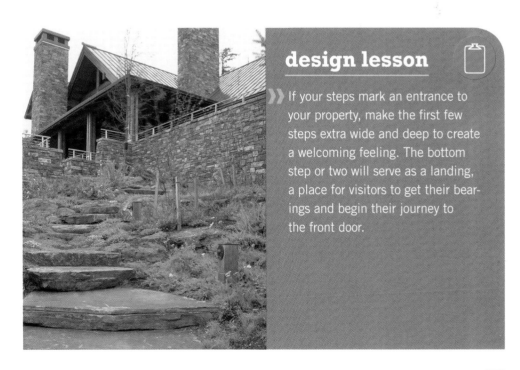

Determining the Number of Steps

Working with a helper, place a long, straight board so it extends horizontally from the top of the slope. When the board is level, measure its height in inches from the bottom of the slope as shown in the illustration. This gives you the overall rise of your staircase. Divide this number by the thickness of the stones you'll be using for your project. Round off the fraction, and you'll have the number of steps you need.

Installing the Steps

Starting at the bottom of the slope, dig a foundation hole as big around as the first stone. Add a 2-inch layer of sand and tamp it firmly with a hand tamper. Move the foundation stone into place and position it so that it slopes slightly downhill and rests about 2 inches above the surrounding soil. Dig back behind the foundation stone to create enough room for the second stone, plus about an inch of sand. Place the next step so that it overlaps the foundation stone by at least 1 inch. Repeat to position other stones. When all the steps are in place, trim back the bank alongside the steps so you can embed some large stones there to keep soil from washing down the steps.

design lesson

>> If your steps mark an entrance to your property, make the first few steps extra wide and deep to create a welcoming feeling. The bottom step or two will serve as a landing, a place for visitors to get their bearings and begin their journey to the front door.

mortared walls

A simple, graceful wall brings order to the surrounding landscape, creating an irresistible focal point.

A mortared stone wall can be narrower than a dry-stacked one and still be strong and stable, but it must rest on a solid concrete footing. Otherwise the mortar joints will crack as the soil heaves in frosts or settles over time. Make sure that your plan for this foundation meets local codes, which take into account regional weather conditions. Once the concrete footing is in place, proceed with the following steps.

① Lay First Course

Mix the mortar. Use a bagged mix or a homemade batch of 1 part masonry cement to 3 parts sand, plus just enough water to make a stiff mixture. Spread a 1-inch layer of mortar on the foundation and set the stones in place. Pack joints with mortar as you go, and wipe up any spilled mortar promptly with a damp sponge.

② Add Stones

Complete the first course, then add more layers. Set three or four stones in place and check that they rest without wobbling, then remove the stones, spread mortar, and replace the stones where they belong. Stagger joints and install bond stones (large enough to span the thickness of the wall) every 6 to 8 feet.

③ Add Filler Stones

Fill gaps larger than 2 inches with small stones rather than mortar. If a stone sinks too deep in the mortar or wobbles, support it in one or two places by tapping in small wooden wedges. After the mortar stiffens, pull out the wedges and pack the holes with mortar.

④ Rake the Joints

When you can press your thumb into the mortar and leave an impression without mortar sticking to your thumb, it's time to rake the joints. Shape the mortar between stones with a small scrap of wood or a pointing tool. If you wish, remove just enough mortar so that it is recessed slightly behind the face of the stones, and work to produce joints that are consistent in depth.

⑤ Finish the Wall

After raking, use a mason's brush to remove all mortar crumbs. If a stone is smeared with mortar, dampen a small towel and scrub the stone. Cover the wall with plastic for several days so that the mortar dries slowly. In dry weather, lift the plastic and mist the wall periodically.

SUNSET HEAD GARDENER RICK LAFRENTZ ON

batter gauges

》 For stability, both sides of a wall should lean inward by 1 to 2 inches for every 2 feet of height. To check this as you build, use a batter gauge made from a carpenter's level, a straight board, and tape.

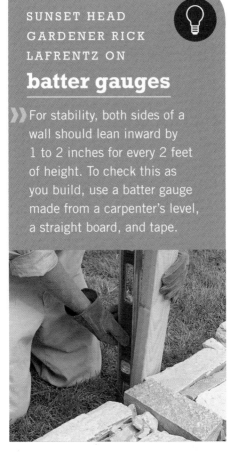

dry-stacked walls

A simple dry-stacked wall separates a path from a planting bed.

Even though it lacks mortar, a freestanding dry-stacked stone wall can be amazingly durable. The key is in the stacking. The wall must be wider at the base than at the top so that each side presses into the other and keeps the wall upright (see the tip on batter gauges on the previous page). Take the time to experiment with different stones and different orientations so that each stone rests solidly in place. Position two stones over one and one stone over two whenever possible. Choose stones that are at least partially squared off and flat on two sides, if possible. Bond stones, long enough to span the thickness of the wall, or at least reach much of the way through it, give the wall much of its strength.

146

❶ Place First Stones Remove

sod and all other organic material from an area about 3 inches wider than the wall's bottom perimeter. Scrape, rather than dig, the bottom of the excavation so that the stones will rest on undisturbed soil. Lay a bond stone at each end of the wall, as well as every 6 to 8 feet along its length. For this course, place the flattest side up. Excavate underneath or add gravel as needed so the stones seat firmly, and fill empty spaces between large stones with tightly packed small stones.

❷ Lay Additional Courses

As you continue to lay stones, keep the courses fairly even. Set large stones on each side and fill in the middle with small stones where needed. To ensure a stable wall, always lay one on top of two rather than stack stones of the same size directly on top of each other. Use a batter gauge to check that the wall leans slightly inward on both sides. Every few courses, add bond stones.

❸ Finish the Wall Gently tap in

small stones to fill gaps in the side of the wall and to keep larger pieces from wobbling. Finish the top with large, flat capstones that overhang the sides of the wall. Test that the capstones are fairly stable when rested on top. Make any necessary adjustments, then mix a batch of mortar and lay a 1- to 2-inch-thick bed. Press the capstones into the mortar.

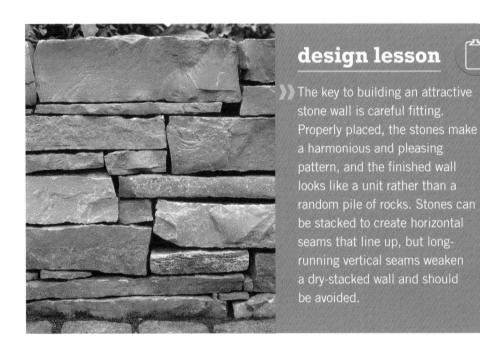

design lesson

❯❯ The key to building an attractive stone wall is careful fitting. Properly placed, the stones make a harmonious and pleasing pattern, and the finished wall looks like a unit rather than a random pile of rocks. Stones can be stacked to create horizontal seams that line up, but long-running vertical seams weaken a dry-stacked wall and should be avoided.

retaining walls

One advantage of a dry-stacked retaining wall over a mortared one is that plants can grow among the wall stones, softening the overall look.

Retaining walls range from hefty structures designed to hold back hillsides to low edging around elevated planting areas. As a do-it-yourselfer, you can reasonably build simple dry-stacked stone walls less than 3 feet tall on a gentle slope with good, stable soil, but be sure to consult with your local building department to determine whether you need a building permit and soil analysis. For more heavy-duty retaining walls, get professional assistance. Dry-stacked stone retaining walls must slope toward the soil they retain, usually by about ¹/₂ to 1 inch per foot. Depending on the weather patterns in your area, you may want to include a drainage pipe behind the wall to speed the process of carrying away rainwater. And if your soil is heavy clay, use landscaping cloth to keep the soil from working its way into the gravel at the back of your wall.

1 Prepare the Site Excavate to attain roughly the slope you need and to create a depression several inches deep along the base of the wall. Nearby, set out the largest stones for the first course. Also stockpile drainage gravel nearby, using pieces of uniform size (without "fines," or small particles). Drive stakes every few feet to establish the approximate front face of the wall.

2 Set the Base Course Place the foundation stones in the shallow excavation and align the front face with the line established by the stakes. Set pieces so they nest well together. If you need to raise an edge, or even an entire stone, fill in with gravel, not soil.

3 Add Gravel When all the foundation stones are in place, step back and check that the front faces create a pleasing line. Make any adjustments, then fill in behind the stones with gravel. From the back, pack the gravel into crevices between the foundation stones and install a drainage pipe, if needed (see page 121).

4 Add Layers Continue adding gravel until it's level with the tops of the foundation stones. Then, starting at the ends or corners and working toward the middle, add a second course, then a third. To keep pieces from wobbling, tap small stones as wedges into the wall from the front or the back. Fill in behind with gravel as you go.

5 Switch to Soil Fill As you near the top of the wall, stop adding gravel backfill. Tuck landscaping cloth, if you are using it, over the top of the gravel and bend it up against the back of the stones. Fill the final inches with soil, packing it firmly.

6 Add the Top Layer This wall has no capstones, but for a tidy look, it still needs a straight top edge. To create a reference line, stake mason's twine at the height you want. Then find stones that are as flat as possible on top and that fit well against adjoining stones.

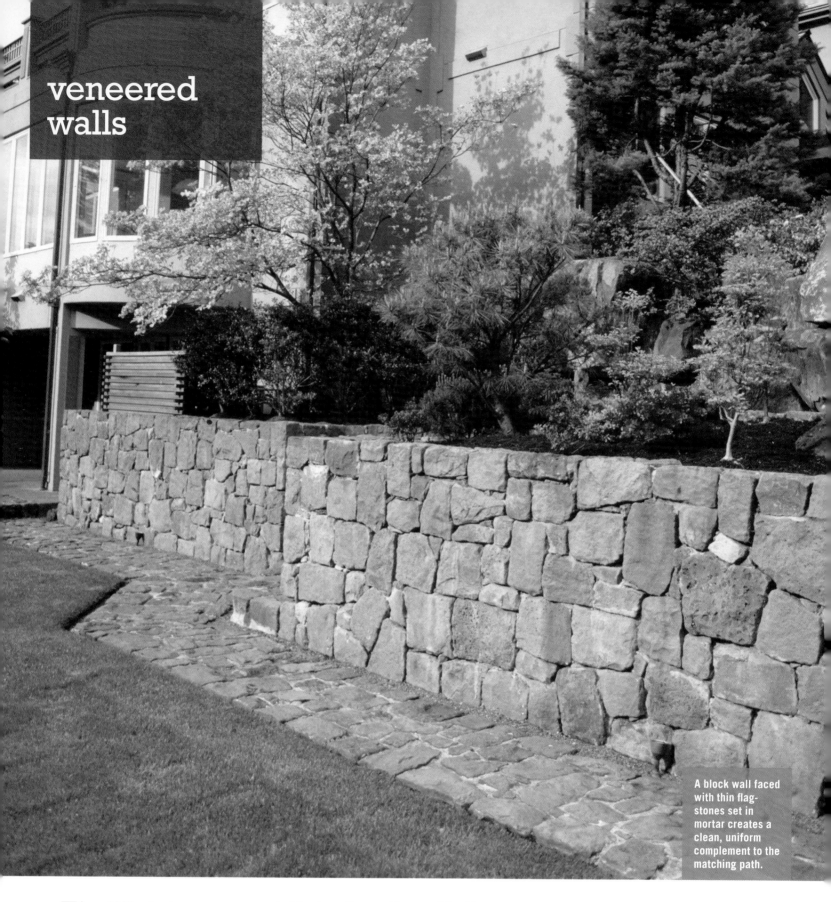

veneered walls

A block wall faced with thin flag-stones set in mortar creates a clean, uniform complement to the matching path.

I f you'd like to dress up a concrete block wall, consider facing it with lightweight veneer stones ranging in thickness from ³⁄₄ to 1³⁄₄ inches. Thin flagstones work well, and other natural-stone veneers are widely avail-able. There are also attractive faux stone veneers manu-factured into uniform shapes; these can closely mimic the look of natural stone. (See page 169 for more about veneer stones.) All are applied in the same basic way.

❶ Plan the Configuration

Lay a sheet of plywood, as wide as the wall is tall, on the ground near the wall and test-fit the stones as they will appear on the wall. Where necessary, cut pieces with a hammer and chisel to make the layout graceful. (You can skip this step if you're using uniformly shaped stone veneer.)

❷ Apply Mortar

Spread a coat of latex bonding agent onto the wall, then mix a batch of mortar. The mortar should be stiff but just wet enough to stick to the stones. Use a straight trowel to apply a thin layer of mortar to the wall.

❸ Set the Bottom Stones

Starting at the bottom, press the stones into the mortar. Where necessary, use blocks of wood to hold the stones in position. Make all adjustments as soon as possible, and avoid moving a stone after the mortar has begun to harden.

❹ Set the Upper Stones

Continue setting stones up to the top of the wall. If the weight of the upper stones causes lower stones to slide down, wait for the mortar to set for the lower stones before installing the upper ones. Make sure at least three quarters of the stone's thickness is embedded in mortar. If not, back-butter stones with mortar before setting them.

❺ Fill and Rake the Joints

After the attachment mortar has hardened, fill the joints. Use a pointed trowel or a mortar bag to press mortar into the joints. Wipe the edges with a damp towel, which you will need to rinse often. When the mortar starts to stiffen, use a pointed trowel to compact mortar in the joints and lift out excess material. Recessing the mortar ½ to ¾ inch adds a nice textural effect. Brush the joints clean.

❻ Cap and Clean the Wall

At the top of the wall, install large stones that overhang the wall by an inch or more on either side. When the mortar has started to harden, gently wash the wall with a little water and a brush, taking care not to wash additional mortar from the joints. Then wipe the wall with a wet towel.

raised beds

A raised bed filled with organically enriched soil provides ideal growing conditions for herbs and vegetables. Sun-warmed stones transfer heat into the soil, so planting can be done earlier.

Here's a quick and fun project that you can easily complete in a weekend. It will fit into a 16-by-16-foot corner of the garden. Use small boulders to create twin raised beds in a circular pattern, leaving room for a comfortably proportioned gravel path between the beds. Each bed is about 11 feet long and 3 feet wide, making it easy to reach the crops inside. Add a gravel path between the beds, then fill the beds with soil and plant herbs and vegetables. Place a stylish birdbath as a centerpiece to attract birds that feed on insects.

1 Design Your Bed Start by laying out your design and deciding which crops you want to grow. Seventeen kinds of herbs and vegetables are shown here, and the Sonoma fieldstones are small enough to be moved easily into place. To make individual stones rest securely, you may need to excavate a small amount of soil. If you wish, cut landscape fabric to fit the path and block weeds; secure the edges beneath the stones.

2 Add Topsoil Once the stones are in place, fill the beds with a rich, fast-draining potting mix. Next, add gravel to the path. For a casual path like the one shown here, a 2-to-3-inch-deep layer of gravel is sufficient. Rake the gravel into a uniform layer and spray lightly with water.

3 Plant the Bed Plant all the herbs and vegetables planned in Step 1. To soften the edges of your raised bed, plant spreading, creeping plants like this oregano, and pack soil between stones so that plants can root there.

SUNSET HEAD GARDENER RICK LAFRENTZ ON

keeping pests at bay

❯❯ If moles or gophers are a problem in your area, install a layer of hardware cloth (wire mesh) beneath the planted areas of your raised beds.

recirculating fountains

Strips of flagstone set on edge form an attractive flat base for a splashy fountain with the look of a natural geyser.

A fountain, by definition, moves water, tossing it into the air or sending it tumbling over an edge. Besides being irresistible to watch, moving water can make a variety of appealing sounds, from the gentle rattle of a pebble fountain to the burble or drip of water spilling on a bed of stones. Electrically powered fountains require a ground-fault-protected (GFCI)— receptacle with a waterproof cover, close enough so you don't need an extension cord. Have your electrician hide the cord and tubing behind stones or plants or run them through a PVC pipe buried in the ground. GFCI outlets should be tested monthly per the manufacturer's instructions and replaced if defective.

INSTALLING A FOUNTAIN   Conceal the works underground.

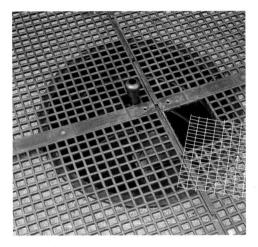

❶ Prepare the Site First, mark the outline of your fountain and remove any sod with a shovel or spade. Then dig a deeper hole for the center basin where your fountain pump will sit, making it slightly wider and deeper than your chosen container.

❷ Install the Basin Add a sufficient amount of sand or gravel to the basin hole to bring the basin to ground level. Place the basin in the hole and check that the rim is level; add or remove sand as needed. To help support the sides, backfill the hole with some of the excavated soil or more sand. Tamp down the sides and check again for level.

❸ Conceal the Pump Place the pump atop a clean brick inside the basin. Take the electrical cable out over the edge of the basin in the direction of the GFCI receptacle; for safety, bury it in PVC conduit. Place the grate over the basin, making sure it overlaps the edges by at least 6 inches. Cut an access hole big enough for your hand so you can reach the pump. Place a square of mesh over the cutout. Fill the basin with water and then cover the grate with your decorative stone. Plug in the pump and adjust the jet spray if necessary.

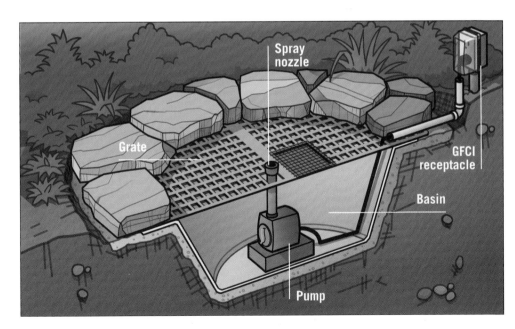

No matter what their design, recirculating fountains generally have the same few working parts: an underground basin that holds water and a pump, a ground-level grate covered with decorative stone, and tubing that leads from the pump to a fountain device, such as a spray nozzle or a spout. The water drains through the stones back into the basin.

garden ponds

Flexible pond liners are easy to install, and a stone edging is a good choice for your pond because it serves two purposes: It gives people a secure place to stand, and it hides edges of the liner. If you plan to add rooting types of water plants, include planting shelves—relatively shallow, flat areas—and grow your plants in pots so that the roots will be just a few inches under the surface. To determine what size liner you'll need, first decide the maximum depth (usually 2 feet) and double it. Then add 2 feet to allow for a 1-foot overlap at the edges and add this total to both the length and the width of your pond. The liner must be at least that big, although it's a good idea to order one a little bigger.

156

❶ Mark and Excavate.
Determine the outline of your pond. A curving, irregular shape looks most natural and is easier to line than one with sharp bends. Mark the outline with a hose or with sand, then use a sharp shovel or spade to dig down to the depth of the planting shelves. Mark the edges of the shelves as you did the perimeter, then dig out the rest of the pond.

❷ Check Level. Set a 2 x 4 across the hole and use a carpenter's level to check for level. If necessary, use some of the excavated soil to build up the low side. Leave the 2 x 4 in place as a guide to measure the depth of the hole and the shelves.

❸ Add Liner Protection.
If you're using liner-protection fabric, install it first. Use stones to hold it in place until the liner is added. An alternative to using liner-protection fabric is to install 2 inches of sand on the bottom and sides of the hole. If you do this, be sure to make the hole a bit deeper to accommodate the sand.

❹ Install the Liner. Drape the liner so that it follows the contours of the hole as closely as possible. Use heavy stones or concrete blocks to hold the edges in place until you are ready to add the water. If you wish, cover the bottom with smooth pebbles or river rocks to conceal and protect the liner.

❺ Fill the Pond. Begin slowly filling the pond with a garden hose. At the same time, start smoothing the liner into shape. Some creases are inevitable, but they can be kept to a minimum with careful fitting and adjusting. Particularly unsightly wrinkles can be covered up later with rocks or plants.

❻ Add the Edging. With the pond nearly filled, begin installing the edging stones. Trim the excess liner, leaving at least 4 to 5 inches beyond the pond's edge. Add edging stones so that they overlap the water by 1 to 2 inches. Seat each one carefully so that it doesn't wobble. Where people will stand, use the largest stones to distribute weight away from the pond's edge.

simple waterfalls

You can adjust the size of the splash and the sound it makes by raising or lowering the stones over which the water falls.

The simplest waterfall is a single-step fall, with the water flowing from a small upper pond to a larger, lower one. Naturally, you'll have an easier time creating such a flow on a site with a bit of a natural slope. The pump for such a water feature sits in the lower pond. Concealed plastic tubing circulates water from the pump back to the upper pond. Have an electrician install a GFCI receptacle in an inconspicuous spot near the lower pond so you can plug in the pump when the project is complete.

❶ Dig the Course

Once you have determined the shape of your water feature, dig holes for the upper and lower ponds. Use excavated soil and small boulders to create a step-like effect along the channel between the two ponds.

❷ Place the Stones

Lay liner-protection fabric and pond liner to cover the entire area (see pages 156–157). Position stones along the edges of the ponds and in the watercourse between them. Place a large, flattish stone at the point of the waterfall, being careful not to tear the liner. Stack taller rocks on each side of the waterfall stone to channel the water and give a sense that water scored a gorge.

❸ Hide the Pump

Attach flexible plastic tubing to the pump. Put the pump in the lower pond and run tubing to the top pond, hiding it under soil, plants, or stones. Fill the ponds with water. Plug in the pump and run the waterfall to check the rock placement and the water's flow and splash.

SUNSET ASSOCIATE GARDEN EDITOR JULIE CHAI ON

preformed liners

❱❱ Instead of piecing together your waterfall with liner and stone, you can buy preformed liners for waterfalls in a number of configurations. Some consist of liners with steps molded in, while others include a holding basin, filtration system, and spillway. These triple-duty products eliminate the need to create an upper pond.

dry creek beds

If there's an area on your property where water flows during rainstorms, build your dry creek bed there so it can do double duty as a drainage channel.

A realistic dry creek conveys a sense of moving water, which always flows in the line of least resistance. Boulders and gravel are placed so as to conjure the idea that the force of water shaped the creek bed. In most streams, there are places where water slows and pools in deep places, and places where it tumbles over rocky shallow stretches or slips through a gorge.

❶ Lay out the Course Using **string or a garden hose,** mark out the course of your dry creek. Curving lines look more natural than straight ones, and it's best to conceal the beginning of the stream behind a large stone or plant. Make some parts wide and others narrow, so that the creek will look like a natural stream.

❷ Excavate a Shallow Bed **Creeks are generally wide and shallow,** so make your creek bed roughly twice as wide as it is deep. Mound the soil on either side of the creek as you work your way along the course. Imitate the way natural streams widen on bends, turning around a rock promontory and leaving a shallow beach downstream on the outside curve.

❸ Line the Bed Lay landscape **fabric over** the streambed to prevent weeds from sprouting. Fold and pleat the cloth as needed where the stream curves, narrows, and widens. Avoid getting soil on the fabric (it can host weeds). Also place any boulders, setting them into depressions dug 1 to 2 inches deep beneath the fabric. Be sure the boulders do not line up in a regimented manner but are spaced naturally.

❹ Add Rocks and Pebbles **Use a variety of stones** to fill the creek bed. Smaller stones can line the sides, and even smaller river-washed pebbles or gravel will help give it the look of water. Partially bury stones along the sides for a more natural look. Near the end of the bed, sprinkle decomposed granite to suggest sediment.

rock gardens

A gentle slope set with boulders makes an ideal location for a rock garden. Plants spill onto the gravel path and occasionally set seed in it.

Rock gardens can be tricky to design because they tend to contain plants that are prone to rot in standard garden beds (see page 173). These plants demand fast-draining soil, yet they still need adequate moisture to thrive. To meet these dual demands, you need to provide four key elements: a slope, a soil mixture that drains fast yet contains a considerable amount of organic matter, a gravel mulch, and rocks spaced so you can plant in gaps where a bit of moisture will linger.

Pick a sunny location exposed to breezes. If you don't have that kind of exposure—such as on a dry bank or a driveway that's cut into a hill—design a low, spreading mound. Remove soil to a depth of at least 18 inches. If you get a lot of summer rain, you may want to install a drainage pipe at the bottom of the hole. Extend the pipe at a downward slope to a dry sink (a hole in the ground filled with rocks), where water can slowly seep into the soil and away from the rock garden.

➊ Work Out a Rough Plan

To get the look of a natural outcropping, place boulders so that their grain or layers run in one direction, and make the tops tilt at a uniform angle. Use stones of different sizes, and vary the spacing between them.

➋ Install Larger Stones and Soil

First place any boulders that you want to rest on the bottom of the excavation or that need to be embedded even deeper. Then spread a 6-inch-thick layer of drainage material over the remaining bottom of the excavation. Use rocks, broken bricks, or chunks of old concrete. Over this rubble, place the remaining large stones. Fill in around them and build up the mound with gritty soil. A typical mix has equal parts loamy topsoil, crushed gravel, and organic material such as leaf mold or compost. You may need to add acidic or alkaline soil amendments to meet the needs of specific plants.

➌ Arrange the Plants

This is best done while they are still in nursery pots. When you like the effect, begin planting, making sure the top of each root ball is about ½ inch above soil level. Then spread 1 or 2 inches of crushed gravel over the entire rock garden, including around the crown of each plant. Water deeply to settle the plants. Choose any size gravel up to ¾ inch in diameter, but avoid mixtures that include extremely fine particles, or "fines," because they pack down too hard. To add plants after the gravel is in place, clear away the gravel mulch so it doesn't get mixed with soil.

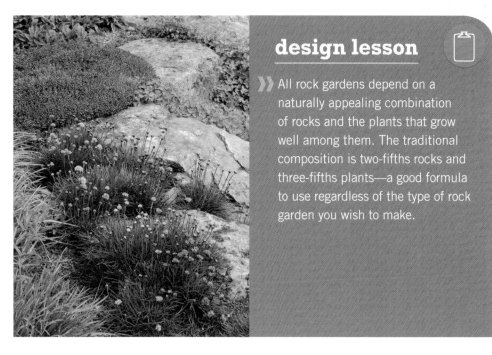

design lesson

》 All rock gardens depend on a naturally appealing combination of rocks and the plants that grow well among them. The traditional composition is two-fifths rocks and three-fifths plants—a good formula to use regardless of the type of rock garden you wish to make.

Finishing the Look

Once you've hit upon the right ideas for stonework in your garden and reviewed the steps and tools you'll need to complete it, you're ready to shop for the raw materials. Before starting construction, however, you may want to consider incorporating lighting to extend the enjoyment of your new garden feature into the evening hours. And of course you'll want to choose the right plants with which to surround your new path, patio, or wall—or to fill that new raised bed or garden pool. In this chapter, you'll find a broad range of options in all of these areas.

A contemporary patio transforms a backyard into an outdoor room outfitted with site-appropriate plants, comfortable seating, and a chic fire bowl that provides light and warmth.

shopping
for stone

Use similar stone for all your garden features, and your landscaping project will look more natural and settled.

On the pages immediately following, you'll find brief descriptions of the various categories of stone, from fine gravels to massive boulders. Familiarize yourself with the terminology, then make a scouting tour of the stone suppliers in your area. Home and garden centers carry some stone products, but stone yards generally have the broadest selection.

Choose local stone whenever possible; it always seems to look right and natural, unlike exotic stone shipped from far away. Local stone is also usually the least expensive because of lower transportation costs, and it tends to be available in many forms—crushed as gravel, squared for blocks, or left in its natural state as large and small boulders.

STONE FOR PATHS AND PATIOS Choose the right paving material for your project.

Stepping-stones

Whether they're flat-topped fieldstones or thick flagstones, stepping-stones have a slightly irregular, nonslip surface and come in manageable sizes, which makes them just right for paths.

Cut Stone

Sometimes called stone tile, this is a formal-looking material suitable for a wide variety of projects. Pieces are cut into squares or rectangles, each with a flat back and sawn edges, and the top surface may be smooth or textured.

Gravel

These small stones are either collected from natural deposits or crushed from larger pieces. Crushed gravel (including very finely ground decomposed granite, or "DG") packs more firmly, making it easier to walk on.

Cobblestones

Usually carved from granite into roughly uniform cubes or brick shapes, cobblestones are easy to work with. They make excellent paths, path edgings, and driveways.

Flagstones

Large, flat slabs of varying thicknesses, flagstones are irregular in shape and often have a slightly rough surface for good traction. For use as stepping-stones or for a patio laid on a sand bed, choose stones that are at least 1½ inches thick. Thinner flagstones will need to be laid in wet mortar or concrete.

Concrete Cobbles

Tumbled and colored to mimic the look of weathered stone, concrete cobblestones are available in various sizes and shapes. You can buy sets to create circular or fan-shaped patterns.

Concrete Pavers

These may be interlocking paving units that resemble bricks or large rectangular, round, or hexagonal pieces with or without exposed aggregate on the surface.

Semi-dressed wall stones stack nicely to form a retaining wall, with plenty of room for tucking plants between stones.

STONES FOR WALLS AND GARDEN FEATURES   Consider workability as well as appearance.

Rubble

These are irregularly shaped wall stones, be they fieldstones or small boulders. They have a natural look, but their random shapes make them a challenging material to build with.

Semi-dressed Stone

These pieces have been roughly trimmed so that they are mostly flat on two sides. This makes them easier to use for building walls, but they still have a rugged, somewhat informal look.

Ashlar

Fully trimmed and formal looking, these block-shaped stones stack easily. The coursed ashlar design shown above features rows of the same height. Other configurations use stones of varying heights.

Natural Veneer Stone

These stones are specially cut into uniformly thick, flat-backed pieces for facing concrete walls. Lightweight, they are easy to set into mortar. They also work well stacked as a low path edging or for building raised beds.

Boulders

This is a general term for a detached and rounded or much-worn piece of rock. A boulder may be a natural fieldstone that was found lying on or buried beneath the soil, a quarried stone that was blasted or excavated from a larger formation, or a large stone that has been smoothed and shaped by water.

Manufactured Veneer Stone

Designed as a facing for stone walls, these are made from lightweight aggregates in panel form or from very thin pieces of natural stone laminated onto composite materials.

River Stones

These have been tumbled and smoothed by flowing water into rounded shapes. Available in a wide variety of sizes and colors, they are especially nice for decorative effects and water features.

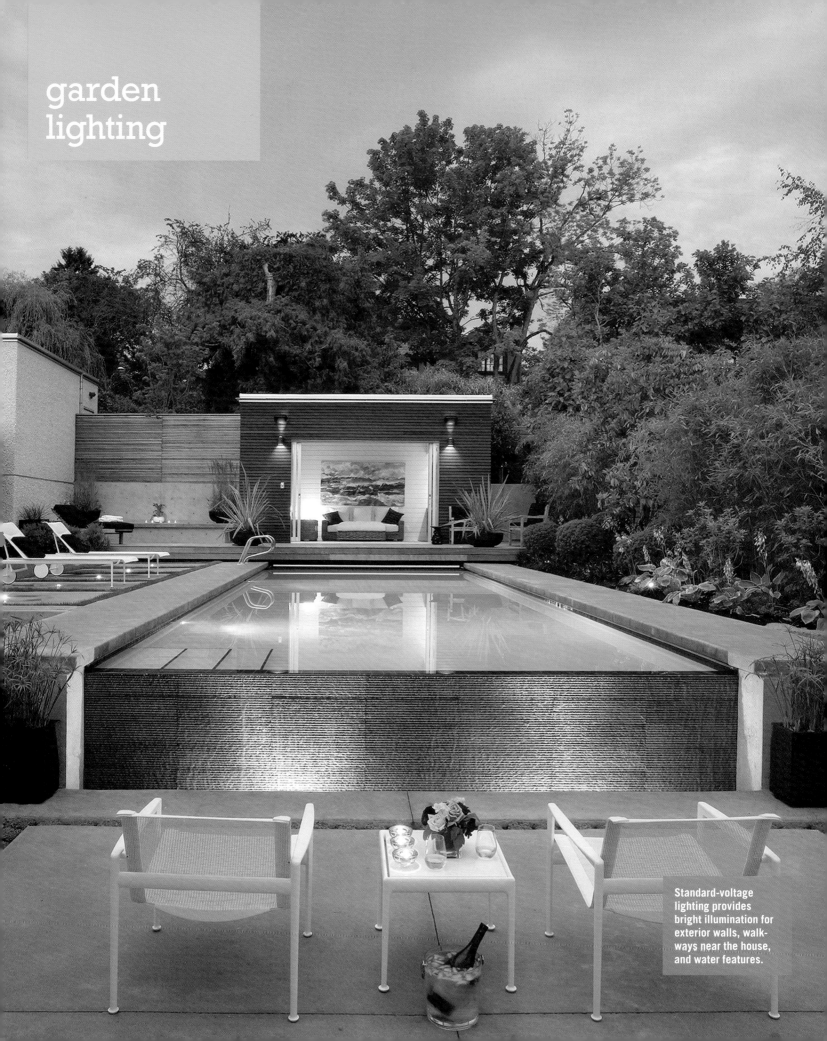

garden
lighting

Standard-voltage lighting provides bright illumination for exterior walls, walkways near the house, and water features.

Spotlights on Path

Highlight your stonework with unobtrusive spotlights set into the wall and trained onto the path (downlighting). Space at regular intervals and stagger on either side of the path so that pools of light barely overlap.

Spotlights in Path

Conceal upward-facing spotlights in a gravel path and train them onto a wall for a dramatic effect. You can also silhouette a tree or shrub by lighting the wall or fence behind it. Be careful not to point the lights so that they shine directly into people's eyes.

Wall-mounted Fixtures

Decorative fixtures like this one add to a wall's appeal day or night. You'll find a broad array of mountable fixtures in every shape, size, and color. Many have built-in sensors that turn on the lights in response to darkness or motion.

Light Posts

Sleek and modern low-voltage fixtures are perfect for spread lighting, which illuminates the surrounding plants as well as the path itself. The type shown here are part of a kit that also includes a programmable transformer and all the necessary cables and connections.

Hanging Lanterns

Lanterns like the ones above can often be found as part of solar-powered systems. These are configured either with panels built into each fixture or with a single remote panel that powers the entire system.

Candlelight

Subtle, elegant, and portable, candles bring romance to the garden. Lanterns may be set along a path or on a table, or hung on trellises or fence hooks. For safety's sake, don't hang lanterns in trees or set them in areas mulched with bark chips.

Nearly covered with plants, this lovely wall and path are completely integrated into the garden.

FOR GARDEN FLOORS   Create a carpet around your stonework.

Filling in Around Stepping-stones

Choose rugged, low-growing plants that can survive the harsh growing conditions around a path—including the occasional footstep—and that stay short enough to be out of the way. Examples include aubrieta, baby's tears, blue star creeper, brass buttons (*Leptinella squalida*), carpet bugle, chamomile, *Dichondra,* dwarf mondo grass, dwarf periwinkle, *Dymondia margaretae,* English daisy, green carpet (*Herniaria glabra*), Irish and Scotch moss, Korean grass (*Zoysia tenuifolia*), *Mazus reptans,* pussy toes, woolly thyme (pictured above), woolly yarrow, and low-growing sedums, speedwells, and violets.

Adding Color Along the Edges

To enliven areas along a path or patio, plant soft-looking, relatively low-growing perennials that flower over a long period. Try African daisy (*Osteospermum*), aster, begonia, blue marguerite (*Felicia amelloides*), chrysanthemum, cinquefoil, sea pink (*Armeria maritima*), common geranium (*Pelargonium*), coral bells, daylily, dead nettle, false spirea (*Astilbe*), gazania, ground morning glory (*Convolvulus sabatius*), lady's-mantle, mounding thymes, *Erigeron,* pansy, petunia, Serbian bellflower, snow-in-summer, cranesbill (*Geranium*), twinspur, and verbena (pictured above). For contrast, add a few small flowering shrubs and spring-blooming bulbs.

Growing in a Gravel Garden

Replace a thirsty lawn or flowerbed with drought-tolerant plants that thrive in sunny, well-drained areas. Try *Agastache,* agave (such as blue *Agave weberi,* pictured above), aloe, Apache plume (*Fallugia paradoxa*), bearded iris, blanket flower, California fuchsia, coreopsis, daffodil, evening primrose (*Oenothera*), gaura, lamb's ears, globe mallow, lavender, love grass (*Eragrostis*), *Muhlenbergia* (such as deer grass, *M. rigens,* pictured above), mullein, needle grass (*Nassella*), penstemon, red valerian, red yucca (*Hesperaloe parviflora*), rock jasmine (*Androsace*), rockrose (*Cistus*), sage, *Santolina, Silene,* stonecrop, verbena, wild buckwheat (*Eriogonum*), yarrow, and yucca.

Keeping Boulders Company

Some plants seem to naturally snuggle up to stones, such as ferns, ornamental grasses, and many bulbs. Low-growing perennials make a stone look more settled, and larger plants grow around a boulder's contours. Other good choices are *Aeonium,* agapanthus, bleeding heart, cinquefoil, daphne, *Echeveria,* gentian, heath (*Erica*), *Sempervivum,* low-growing junipers, meadowsweet (*Filipendula*), *Phlomis* (such as Jerusalem sage, *P. fruticosa,* pictured above), pink (*Dianthus*), rockrose (*Cistus*), Russian sage (*Perovskia*), Scotch heather, St. Johnswort, sunrose (*Helianthemum nummularium*), cranesbill (*Geranium*), and wallflower (*Erysimum*).

design lesson

》 Reflected heat from stones and the limited amount of soil and water available in the planting spaces make getting plants started a challenge between stone paving pieces. Buy small, young plants and keep them well watered until they are established. In hot weather, you may need to erect shade cloth over the plants. If the plants fail, try sowing seed in the gaps.

Spilling over a Wall

To soften the edge, install plants just above a retaining wall. Look for quick-growing perennials and annuals with a spreading or low, mounding shape, such as aubretia, bacopa, basket-of-gold (*Aurinia saxatilis*), creeping baby's breath (*Gypsophila repens*), creeping Jenny, dwarf morning glory (*Convolvulus tricolor*), dwarf periwinkle, English ivy, *Erigeron*, evergreen candytuft, garden nasturtium, *Impatiens walleriana,* ivy geranium (*Pelargonium*), licorice plant, *Lobelia erinus* (trailing types), *Lotus*, million bells, rose moss (*Portulaca grandiflora*), *Saponaria*, *Scaevola*, Serbian bellflower, strawberry geranium (*Saxifraga stolonifera*), Swan river daisy (*Brachyscome*), sweet alyssum, and trailing types of petunia, twinspur, and verbena. Or plant low-growing, spreading shrubs like cotoneaster (some), *Euonymus fortunei,* juniper (some), trailing lantana, lavender, ground-cover roses, Australian bluebell creeper (*Sollya heterophylla*), or prostrate rosemary.

Growing Alongside Stairs

The ideal step-side plants have dense, wide-spreading roots that knit the soil. It's also a plus when the plants are attractive from either above or below. Choices include artemisia, Australian fuchsia (*Correa*), bamboo (pictured above), bottlebrush (*Callistemon*), breath of heaven (*Coleonema*), cape plumbago, cotoneaster, crape myrtle, flowering quince, forsythia, heath, manzanita, ninebark (*Physocarpus*), ornamental grasses, Pride of Madeira (*Echium candicans*), pyracantha, rockrose (*Cistus*), rosemary, snowberry (*Symphoricarpos*), salal (*Gaultheria shallon*), santolina, shrubby dogwoods (*Cornus*), toyon (*Heteromeles arbutifolia*), and Zabel laurel. Many climbing vines (see next list) will also scramble nicely down hillsides.

Climbing a Wall

Some attach themselves firmly to a wall with sucker-like holdfasts or aerial roots; often called clinging vines, these include climbing hydrangea, creeping fig, ivy, and *Parthenocissus*. Other vines scramble and clamber up a wall, leaning against it and perhaps twining around or hooking onto protrusions with their tendrils. Some favorite choices in this category are Carolina jessamine (*Gelsemiium sempervirens*), cat's claw (*Macfadyena unguis-cati*), clematis, climbing roses, honeysuckle, morning glory (pictured above), nasturtium, ornamental grape (*Vitis*), and sweet pea.

Filling Wall Crevices

A surprising variety will grow well in the niches of dry-laid walls. To get them started, line the largest gaps with sphagnum moss, fill with soil, plant, and water lightly. Choose small ferns for a wall that's shaded, and encourage moss with occasional misting. For walls in the sun, the many choices include cheddar pink (*Dianthus gratianopolitanus*), cranesbill (*Geranium*) (small types), Dalmatian bellflower (*Campanula portenschlagiana*), *Euphorbia myrsinites*, *Echeveria*, globe daisy, houseleek (*Sempervivum*), ice plant, *Lewisia*, oregano (creeping types), rockcress (*Arabis*), Santa Barbara daisy, sea pink (*Armeria maritima*), sedum, Spanish lavender (small varieties), stonecress (*Aethionema*), trailing phlox (*Phlox nivalis*), and small thymes.

Shading a Patio

Small, well-behaved trees make an outdoor room cozier. Look for trees that have noninvasive roots and do not drop a lot of litter. Top choices among deciduous trees, which offer shade in the warm months but let in more light in winter, include crape myrtle, dogwood, flowering cherry, flowering crabapple, juneberry (*Amelanchier*), small magnolias, small maples, palo verde (*Cercidium*), Persian parrotia, redbud, smoke tree (*Cotinus*), sourwood, and stewartia. Evergreen patio trees provide year-round shade; best bets include bronze loquat, citrus, small types of cypress, *Michelia*, fruitless forms of olive, smaller palms, fern pine (*Podocarpus*) and evergreen pear.

Growing in Patio Containers

Trees and shrubs that grow well in pots and planters are not as easy to find as container-suitable annuals, perennials, herbs and vegetables. Here are some of your best bets for large containers: Angel's trumpet (*Brugmansia*), apple (dwarf), azalea, bamboo, boxwood, citrus, camellia, flowering maple (*Abutilon*), frangipani (*Plumeria*), gardenia, heavenly bamboo (*Nandina domestica*), holly (some), hydrangea (smaller varieties), Japanese aucuba, Japanese auralia (*Fatsia japonica*), Japanese maple, Japanese privet, lavender, peach (dwarf), lily-of-the-valley shrub (*Pieris*), pomegranate (dwarf), rhododendron, rose, sago palm, sweet bay (*Laurus nobilis*), winter daphne (*Daphne odora*), and yucca.

Planting Near a Fire Feature

There's no such thing as a fireproof plant, but some are slower to ignite than others. Always keep any plants growing near a fire feature well watered and pruned. Among slower-to-burn trees are aspen (*Populus*), Incense cedar (*Calocedrus decurrens*), maple, birch, flowering dogwood, sweetgum (*Liquidambar*), apple, cherry, oak, and willow. Shrubs that are less likely to catch fire include azalea, butterfly bush, cotoneaster, lavender, lemon bottlebrush (*Callistemon citrinus*), *Mahonia*, monkeyflower (*Mimulus*), *Philadelphus*, privet (*Ligustrum*), saltbush (*Atriplex*), serviceberry (*Amelanchier*), rhododendron, toyon (*Heteromeles arbutifolia*), and yucca. Good choices among perennials include yarrow, bergenia, coreopsis, cranesbill (*Geranium*), daylily, coral bells, hosta, iris, penstemon, and lamb's ears. Less-flammable groundcovers include carpet bugle, dusty miller (*Senecio cineraria*), dwarf periwinkle, ice plant (*Delosperma*), kinnikinnick (*Arctostaphylos uva-ursi*), ornamental strawberry (*Fragaria*), sedum, snow-in-summer, St. Johnswort (*Hypericum calycinum*), winter creeper (*Euonymus fortunei*), and woolly yarrow.

Growing Near a Swimming Pool

When choosing plants for the pool or spa area, look for ones that drop very little litter; any leaves or spent flowers they do shed should be too large to enter the pool's filter. And to protect bare skin, avoid plants with sharp leaves, thorns, or bristles. Consider camellia, *Aeonium*, *Agave attenuata*, bird of paradise, canna, *Cyperus*, daylily, edible fig, elephant's ear, fortnight lily (*Dietes*), ginger lily (*Hedychium*), honey bush (*Melianthus*), hydrangea, jade plant, Japanese auralia (*Fatsia japonica*), kangaroo paw (*Anigozanthos*), lily turf (*Liriope*), New Zealand flax, ornamental banana, palms, pineapple guava, tobira (*Pittosporum tobira*), *Schefflera*, sea lavender (*Limonium perezii*), Texas olive (*Cordia boissieri*), and tree ferns.

Growing Alongside a Dry Creek Bed

In a natural creek bed, grasses and other plants with thin, reed-like leaves grow along the banks, punctuated by flowering or leafy plants, some of which cascade toward the water. For a dry creekbed, you want to get the same look—but with drought-tolerant plants. For the grassy look, use fountain grass (*Pennisetum setaceum*), lyme grass (*Leymus*), *Muhlenbergia*, *Nassella*, red yucca (*Hesperaloe parviflora*), *Sporobolus*, or *Stipa gigantea*. Then fill in with drought-tolerant partner plants like agapanthus, *Agastache*, agave, artemisia, bearded iris, blackfoot daisy (*Melampodium leucanthum*), coreopsis, evening primrose (*Oenothera*), gazania, New Zealand flax, *Opuntia*, penstemon, *Protea*, red valerian (*Centranthus ruber)*, rosemary, Santa Barbara daisy, sea lavender (*Limonium perezii*), and yarrow.

Edging a Stream

Plants that thrive with lots of water but also appreciate good drainage are ideal for areas directly adjacent to a waterfall or stream. Among the many choices are Bowles' golden grass (*Milium effusum* 'Aureum'), calla lily, ferns (most), fiber optics plant (*Isolepis cernua*), globeflower (*Trollius*), *Gunnera*, hosta, iris Louisiana, and Siberian, Joe-pye weed (*Eupatorium purpureum*), meadowsweet (*Filipendula*), moor grass (*Molinia caerulea*), New England aster, ornamental rhubarb (*Rheum*), primrose (some), *Rodgersia*, rush (*Juncus*), scarlet monkey flower (*Mimulus cardinalis*), sedge (*Carex*), sweet flag (*Acorus*), switch grass (*Panicum virgatum*), turtlehead (*Chelone lyonii*), umbrella plant (*Darmera peltata*).

Growing in a Pond

Two types of aquatic plants grow well in submerged pots. Floating-leaf plants are rooted in soil, but their leaves—and lovely flowers, in many cases—float on the surface. These include floating heart (*Nymphoides*), lotus, water clover (*Marsilea*), water hawthorn (*Aponogeton distachyus*), water lily, and water poppy (*Hydrocleys nymphoides*). The second group comprises marginal or bog plants, which rise to or above the surface from their pots. Look for blue flag (*Iris versicolor*), canna, cape rush (*Chondropetalum elephantinum*), cattail (*Typha*), *Cyperus*, horsetail (*Equisetum hyemale*, pictured above), Japanese iris, marsh marigold (*Caltha palustris*), parrot feather, pickerel weed (*Pontaderia cordata*), primrose (some), taro, and yellow flag (*Iris pseudacorus*)

Floating on a Pond

Aquatic plants that float in the water with their roots dangling free can be the finishing touch for a pond garden. Shop for fairy moss (*Azolla caroliniana*), frogbit (*Hydrocharis morsus-ranae*), water fern (*Salvinia minima*), water hyacinth (*Eichhornia crassipes*, pictured above), or water lettuce (*Pistia stratiotes*).

SUNSET GARDEN EDITOR
KATHLEEN NORRIS BRENZEL ON

invasive aquatics

>> Many aquatic plants—especially free-floating types—reproduce quickly and may need to be thinned occasionally to keep them from overcrowding your pond. Their enthusiastic growth can spell trouble if these plants escape into waterways near your home. Check with your county agricultural extension agent (cxrees.usda.gov) about which aquatic plants pose such a risk.

Seek professional advice or help before installing a complex, multi-level stonescape such as this one, where proper drainage is especially important.

M any of the simpler stonescaping features shown in this book—such as stepping-stone paths, low raised beds, or even small recirculating fountains—can be constructed by do-it-yourselfers in a weekend or two. Refer to chapter 2 for a range of such straightforward projects. Larger stonescaping projects, such as pools, sizeable patios, and extensive walls, will almost certainly require the assistance of a landscape professional. But before you seek help, familiarize yourself with the different categories of landscape pros.

Landscape Architects

Plant experts who are also licensed to design exterior structures, landscape architects solve complicated drainage and elevation problems and give advice on where to place service lines, entries, driveways, and parking areas.

Landscape Designers or Garden Designers

These design specialists may be self-taught or may have the same academic credentials as a landscape architect but do not have a state license. They are more likely to work on smaller, strictly residential projects.

Licensed Landscape Contractors

Contractors are trained in methods of earthmoving, construction, and planting. They may subcontract specialty jobs like electrical work, water feature installation, or wall building.

Stonemasons and Bricklayers

These artisans are trained in the special skills needed to build with stone and brick.

Horticulturists

Skilled in the selection and care of garden plants, horticulturists can also give valuable input regarding preparation of soil before planting.

Before your first meeting with a professional, start making an idea file with photos, sketches, plant preferences, and any other information that might help the designer or landscape architect understand what you hope to achieve. Ask to see samples of finished projects so you can evaluate the quality of their work and better understand their sense of design. Even if you're planning on doing the work yourself, it's a good idea to consult a professional to make sure you fully understand what's involved. A poorly designed structure or drainage system may have serious—and expensive—consequences down the road.

keeping it green

By using recycled landscape timbers for steps and local stone for the wall and flagstone path, the homeowners reduced the impact of their project on the environment.

Landscaping with stone can be eco-friendly, particularly if you keep in mind a few suggestions for conserving resources and protecting the environment. Once in place, most stone-work requires no maintenance or resources to stay great looking year-round.

» Use stone from the nearest source. If you have stones on your property, use them. Otherwise, choose stones collected or quarried locally to cut down on fuel used for transport.

» If you have a lawn, reduce its size by adding a patio or even just a pathway along one side. Or replace this resource-gobbling feature altogether with a gravel garden or a path through beds of low-maintenance plants.

» Opt for low-voltage or solar-powered lighting and fountains.

» Choose natural gas for your outdoor fireplace, fire pit, or grill. It burns more cleanly than wood.

» To reduce wasteful runoff, choose permeable paving materials such as open-cell driveway paving systems or stepping-stone paths set in gravel.

» Set lights or running fountains on timers. For lights, consider daylight-sensitive photocells or motion-sensor fixtures.

» Use a broom to clean your patio, driveway, or path, rather than a jet of water from the hose.

» Be sure to grade for on-site drainage, and consider adding a French drain, dry creek bed, or series of terraces to prevent runoff.

» Reuse old bricks, broken concrete, and other hardscape materials whenever possible. Filling a gabion wall with recycled materials is one good option.

» Install a cover for your swimming pool. This will reduce the energy needed for heating, cut down on evaporation, and minimize the amount of chemicals needed.

» When it's time to plant, choose low-maintenance plants that won't need constant watering, pruning, and spraying with chemicals to look good. Consider using plants native to your area, as they are well adapted to the natural conditions.

TOP: Drought-tolerant, low-maintenance plants like this tall Mexican weeping bamboo, fortnight lily (left) and agave (lower right) combine beautifully with a simple gravel path.

BOTTOM: This stony backyard features a fire ring set at ground level and fueled by natural gas, which burns much more cleanly than wood.

resource guide

The following list is of organizations, manufacturers, and retailers that you might find helpful in creating your new patio or stonescape, with an emphasis on companies dedicated to environmentally responsible manufacturing processes and products. To find a local source for stone, check online sources listed here for local dealers or look in the Yellow Pages under these headings: Stone—Natural, Stone—Landscaping, Quarries, Rock, Building Materials, Landscape Equipment and Supplies.

Organizations and Associations

American Society of Landscape Architects
www.asla.org
202-898-2444, 888-999-2752

Association of Professional Landscape Designers
www.apld.com
717-238-9780

The Association of Pool and Spa Professionals
www.apsp.org
703-838-0083

Building Materials Reuse Association
www.buildingreuse.org
800-990-2672

The Masonry Advisory Council
www.maconline.org
847-297-6704
Provides information about masonry design and detail

North American Rock Garden Society
www.nargs.org

Stonescaping Products

Allan Block Corporation
www.allanblock.com
952-835-5309
Stackable block for retaining walls and vertical walls

Buechel Stone Corporation
www.buechelstone.com
800-236-4473
Quarried limestone for building and landscaping

Butterfield Color
www.butterfieldcolor.com
800-282-3388
Concrete colorant, stains, stamps

The Colonial Stoneyard
www.thecolonialstoneyard.com
978-448-3329
Natural stone and stone products for landscaping

Concrete Art
www.concreteart.net
800-500-9445
Decorative scoring and staining system

Coverall Stone, Inc.
www.coverallstone.com
800-779-3234
Natural stone columns, tiles, pebbles, fountains, benches

Cultured Stone
www.culturedstone.com
800-255-1727
Manufactured stone

D. A. Spencer Natural Stone Water Sculptures, Inc.
www.naturalstonewater
sculptures.com
585-924-7542
Hand-carved stone sculptures

EP Henry Corporation
www.ephenry.com
800-444-3679
Concrete pavers, blocks, veneers

Goshen Stone Co., Inc.
www.goshenstone.com
413-268-7171
Natural stone

High Plains Stone
www.highplainsstone.com
303-791-1862
Building, masonry, and landscaping stone

Hi-Tech Architectural Products
www.granitepaving.com
Granite and concrete cobbles and pavers

The Home Depot
www.homedepot.com
Building and landscaping materials, patio furnishings

Lang Stone Company
www.langstone.com
800-589-5264
Full range of natural stone products

Little Meadows Stone Co.
www.littlemeadowsstone.com
866-305-3250
Natural Pennsylvania landscape stone

Lowe's Home Improvement
www.lowes.com
Building and landscaping materials, patio furnishings

Lyngso Garden Materials, Inc.
www.lyngsogarden.com
650-364-1730
Natural stone, construction materials

L & W Stone Corporation
www.lwstonecorp.com
800-346-9739
Natural stone pavers, boulders, veneer

Paver Search
www.paversearch.com
Paver products and resources

Robinson Brick
www.robinsonbrick.com
800-477-9002
Brick and thin true-stone veneer

StoneDeck West, Inc.
www.stonedeckwest.com
877-686-4759
Natural stone decking systems

Sure-loc Edging
www.surelocedging.com
800-787-3562
Aluminum and steel landscape and paver edging

The Stone Yard
www.stoneyard.com
800-231-2200
Natural building and landscaping stone

Mail-Order Sources for Rock-Garden Plants

Arrowhead Alpines
www.arrowhead-alpines.com
517-223-3581

Avant Gardens
www.avantgardensne.com
508-998-8819

Beaver Creek Greenhouses
www.rockgardenplants.com

Evermay Nursery
www.evermaynursery.com
207-827-0522

Siskiyou Rare Plant Nursery
www.siskiyourareplant
nursery.com
541-535-7103

Sunscapes Rare Plant Nursery
www.sunscapes.net
719-546-0047

Trennoll Nursery
PO Box 125
Trenton, OH 45067-1614
513-988-6121

Wild Ginger Farm
www.wildgingerfarm.com
503-632-2338

Patio Furniture and Accessories

All-Safe Pool Safety Barriers
www.allsafepool.com
800-786-8110
Pool fences, safety-net pool covers

Allsop Home Garden
www.allsopgarden.com
866-425-5767
Solar lanterns and garden art

The Blue Rooster Company
www.thebluerooster.com
800-303-4312
Chimeneas and fire pits

Garden-Fountains.com
www.garden-fountains.com
Outdoor fountains, statuary, and accents

Hyannis Country Garden
www.countrygarden.com
508-775-8703
Water gardening supplies

Iron Age Designs
www.ironagegrates.com
206-276-0925
Drain and tree grates and architectural castings

Kinetic Fountains.com
www.kineticfountains.com
Recirculating fountains and accessories

Patiolife.com
www.patiolife.com
Outdoor and patio furniture

Restoration Hardware
www.restorationhardware.com
800-910-9836
Outdoor furniture and umbrellas

Sunbrella
www.sunbrella.com
336-221-2211
Outdoor fabric

Whit McLeod
www.whitmcleod.com
707-822-7307
Outdoor furniture made from reclaimed lumber

Outdoor Kitchens

Barbeques Galore
www.bbqgalore.com
800-752-3085
Barbecues and accessories

Fogazzo Wood Fired Ovens and BBQs
www.fogazzo.com
866-364-2996

Marvel Scientific
www.marvelscientific.com
800-962-2521
Outdoor refrigerators

Weber-Stephen Products Co.
www.weber.com
800-446-1071
Outdoor appliances and accessories

glossary

Aggregate Small, round stones, often of various colors, that are seeded into wet concrete to make an attractive surface.

Alpine plants Plants native to mountain slopes above the tree line. Good for rock gardens, as they typically require quick drainage and lean soil.

Ashlar Square-cut stone that can be laid in courses like brick.

Backfill Soil that has been dug out from one spot and filled into another; may also refer to gravel, sand, or crushed stone used for the same purpose. It doesn't offer the uniform support of undisturbed earth.

Batter The inward tilting of the face of a stone wall; it improves the wall's structural stability.

Bond stone, or tie stone A large stone that extends through the thickness of a stone wall, tying the faces together. Sometimes called a through stone.

Capstone Stone laid as the top course of a wall.

Cement, portland A manufactured product, a basic ingredient in both mortar and concrete.

Cobblestones Roughly cut stone blocks, once used for street paving; can be laid like cut stone.

Concrete A mixture of sand, gravel or crushed rock, portland cement, and water; when cured, it forms a solid material.

Coping Flat stone used to make a finished top to a wall or a neat edge to a pool.

Course A single horizontal layer of stones in a stone wall.

Crazy paving Paving made of irregularly shaped flagstone.

Curing Keeping mortar or concrete moist for several days while it hardens.

Cut stone Sawn rectangles and squares of stone that are flat on one or both sides.

Decomposed granite Naturally broken stone particles ranging in size from small gravel to sand.

Dressed stone Stone that has been squared off on all sides and has at least one smooth face.

Dry-stacked wall A stone wall built without mortar; it depends upon the weight and friction of one stone on another for stability.

Excavation The removal of soil, often done so that paving will have a hard, uniform surface upon which to rest.

Face The exposed side of a stone.

Fieldstone Stones culled from fields or old walls, irregular in shape and size with aged, uncut faces.

Flagstone A generic term for flat slabs of paving stone, usually sandstone, limestone, or slate, which split easily; it may have irregular edges or be cut into squares and rectangles.

Footing A below-ground concrete slab or gravel-bed foundation that supports a stone wall.

Form A wooden frame built to contain cast concrete while it hardens.

Frost heave The movement in soil caused by the soil water alternately freezing and thawing.

Frost line The depth to which soil freezes in winter.

Gravel Two kinds: small naturally round stones, like pea gravel, suitable only for a paving surface; and mechanically crushed stone, in various small sizes, suitable for path surfaces and for foundations beneath paths and dry-stone wall foundations because it packs well.

Ground-fault circuit interrupter, GFI or GFCI, receptacle Electrical receptacle with a circuit designed to break, within $\frac{1}{40}$ of a second, if a leak develops in the current; fitted with waterproof cover for outdoor uses.

Hardscape The material in a landscape that is not living, such as stone, lumber, or concrete.

Liner-protection fabric A nonwoven geotextile that is extremely resistant to tearing.

Mortar The "glue" used to bond stones together; typically composed of water, lime or fireclay, portland cement, and sand. Mortar can stain stone, so clean up spills quickly.

Muriatic acid solution Removes mortar smears but may change the color of the stone; don't use on limestone or marble. Prepare with caution, wearing rubber gloves, goggles, and mask; add acid slowly to water—never the reverse.

Paver Stones trimmed to a uniform size and shape, typically used for paths and patios.

Quarried rock Stone with raw, broken surfaces, suitable mostly for functional paving and walls.

Retaining wall A wall that holds back sloping ground.

River rock Stone made smooth by the action of water; ranges in size from gravel to small boulders.

Rubble stone Any type of uncut stone; it is used in walls but is too irregular to lay in courses.

Runoff Rainwater or irrigation water moving over the soil or paving surface.

Screeding Moving a straight board, called a screed, back and forth across the top of a framing form to smooth and level concrete or sand inside the form.

Stretcher stones Long stones that are laid, a few to every course, on the face of a wall.

Tamp To compact sand, gravel, or soil using the back of a spade, a metal tamper, a water-fillable drum roller, or a rented power vibrator.

Threshold stone A large or attractive stone at the beginning of a path or at a path intersection.

Veneer stone Split stone or manufactured stone-like material that is used to give a stone face to a concrete block wall.

photography credits

Karen Aitken: 72 (design: Aitken & Associates); courtesy of Ames True Temper: 126 top row #4, 126 bottom row #2; James Baigrie/Getty Images: 175 left; Red Cover/Christine Bauer: 39; Botanica/JupiterImages: 162, 172; Brand X Pictures/Getty Images: 127 bottom row, #1; Marion Brenner: 21, 23 top (design: Ronn Mann Design), 24 bottom, 31, 34 top left, 34 top right, 35, 37 top left, 38 all, 41 top, 44 bottom (design: Laura White and Jude Hellewell, Outer Space Landscape Architecture), 48 top right (design: Patricia Wagner Garden Design), 53 bottom, 60–61, 61 top, 65 both, 66, 70–71, 75, 80, 81, 83 bottom, 84 bottom, 84–85, 91 top left, 93, 99 bottom, 100 bottom, 113 top, 114, 117, 138, 144, 146, 148, 156, 157 all, 160–161 (design: Roger Warner Design), 173 #4, 177 right, 180–181; Rob D. Brodman: 24 top left (design: Cathy Drees, Accent Gardens), 32–33 (design: Windsmith Design), 43 (design: Shari Bashin-Sullivan and Richard Sullivan), 82–83 (design: Windsmith Design), 137 all, 152, 153 top middle, 153 top right, 171 bottom row #3 (design: Jon Buerk, J. Buerk Landscape/Maintenance), back cover bottom (Windsmith Design); Jonathan Buckley/The Garden Collection: 176 right (design: Alana Titchmarsh); Sharyn Cairns/acpsyndication.com/JBG Photo: 8; Jennifer Cheung: 6 (landscape designer: Amelia B. Lima), 33 top (design: Brian Kissinger), 36 (design: Brian Kissinger), 94 top right; Peter Christiansen: 167 bottom row #1; Creative Crop/Getty Images: 127 top row #1; Sue Daley + Steve Gross: 174 left; Francois De Heel/Photolibrary: 171 top row #2; Andrew Drake: 147 bottom; Miki Duisterhof/Botanica/Jupiterimages: 26; John Durant: 109 right; Catriona Tudor Erler: 159 bottom; Red Cover/Ron Evans: 7 bottom, 47 top; **Sue Ferris/acpsyndication. com/JBG Photo:** 77 bottom; **Scott Fitzgerrell:** 126 top row #2, 126 top row #3; **Roger Foley:** front cover (design: Tom Mannion, Landscape Design), 10–11 (design: Armstrong-Berger), 63 (design: Tom Mannion Landscape Design), 71 bottom (landscape architect: Yunghi Cho), 104 top right (design: Oehme, van Sweden & Associates); **Frank Gaglione:** 125 top left, 125 top middle, 126 bottom row #1, 126 bottom row #3, 127 middle row #1, 127 middle row #3, 127 bottom row #3, 145 bottom, 147 top left, 147 top middle, 147 top right, 151 all, 167 top row #4, 167 bottom row #2, 169 top row #1, 169 top row #2, 169 top row #3, 169 bottom row #3; **Tria Giovan:** 174 right; **Red Cover/Tria Giovan:** 88 top right, 190; **Andrea M. Gómez:** 173 #1; **Gross + Daley:** 13; **Steven A. Gunther:** 15 top (design: Margaret Grace, Grace Design Associates), 15 bottom (design: Mia Lehrer, Mia Lehrer + Associates), 16 (design: Michael Buccino, Michael Buccino Associates), 19, 25 (design: Nancy Goslee Power & Associates), 30 (design: Ellen Speert, California Center for Creative Renewal), 33 bottom (design: Nancy Goslee Power & Associates), 44 top right (Mary Rose Duffield, Duffield Ratliff Landscape Design; Rosalee Gage, formerly of Santa Rita Landscaping), 52–53 (design: Gary Marsh, Gary Marsh Design; plantings: Tom Henthorne, Henthorne Landscape Design), 61 bottom (design: Margaret West, Margaret West Design), 67 (design: Rich Grigsby, The Great Outdoors Landscape Design), 77 top, 87, 91 bottom, 96 (design: Steve Martino), 97, 98–99, 99 top, 104 top left, 105, 107 bottom, 110 (design: Jeffrey Gordon Smith), 122, 128, 134 (design: Elysian Landscapes), 154 (design: Mark Bartos and Tony Exter of BEM Design Group), 164–165 (design:

Griffith & Cletta); **Jamie Hadley:** 155 all; **Jerry Harpur, Harpur Garden Images:** 24 top right (design: Tom-Stuart-Smith), 37 bottom, 68 top right (design: Christoper Bradley-Hole), 69 (design: Gary Searle), 100 top right (design: Jarrod Marsden and Robert Wilberfoss), 102 (design: Tom Stuart-Smith), 111 right (owners: Mr. and Mrs. Lunn), 188 (La Casella, France); **Marcus Harpur, Harpur Garden Images:** 11 bottom (design: Nick Williams-Ellis), 24 top right, 29 bottom (owners: Mr. and Mrs. Brighten), 48 top left (design: Geoffrey Whiten), 104 bottom (design: Arabella Lennox-Boyd), 168 (design: Jamie Dunstan), 178 right (design: Mamey Hall, RHS Chelsea 2003); **Philip Harvey:** 127 top row #2, 127 top row #3, 167 top row #3, 169 bottom row #1; **Saxon Holt:** 40–41 (design: Nancy Driscoll), 68 bottom, 73, 84 top, 125 bottom (design: Suzanne van Atta), 131 (design: Suzanne Arca), 171 top row #3, 179 right; **D. A. Horchner:** 41 bottom (design: Faith Okuma, formerly of Design Workshop); **iStockphoto. com:** 127 top row #5, 127 top row #6, 127 top row #7; **Jon Jensen:** 5 (landscape contractor: Dean DeSantis, DeSantis Landscapes; Timber-frame construction: Jim DeSantis, Silver Creek Timber Works), 42 (landscape contractor: Dean DeSantis, DeSantis Landscape; timber-frame construction: Jim DeSantis, Silver Creek Timber Works), 78 top left; **Jetta Productions/Getty Images:** 123; **Red Cover/Jumping Rocks:** 111 left; **ND Koster Photography:** 88 top left (Design: Tom Wilhite); **Chuck Kuhn:** 149 all, 167 bottom row #3; **Holly Lepere:** 37 top right (design: Margaret Grace, Grace Design Associate), 101, back cover top right; **Derek Lepper:** 170 (design: Cameron Owen, IBI Group); **Chris Leschinsky:** 11 top (Ryan Fortini Design Group), 20 (design: Jeffrey Gordon Smith

Landscape Architecture), 28–29 (design: Jeffrey Gordon Smith), 175 right; **Jason Liske:** 68 top left (design: Bernard Trainor + Associates); **Janet Loughrey:** 12 (design: Penny Vogel and Millie Kiggins), 173 #2; **Richard Maack:** 83 top; **Allan Mandell:** 86 (design & stonework: Jeff Bale), 140 (design: Vanessa Nagel, Milieux Design Studio); **Jean Maurice/ Getty Images:** 27; **Red Cover/ Simon McBride:** 51; **Ericka McConnell:** 55; **Joe McDonald/ Getty Images:** 153 bottom; **Maura McEvoy/Getty Images:** 171 bottom row #2; **Red Cover/ Karyn Millet:** 23 bottom; **Minh+ Wass/StockFood:** 59 bottom; **Red Cover/James Mitchell:** 44 top left, 171 top row #1; **Jerry Pavia:** 71 top, 90, 94 bottom, 143, 150; **Red Cover/Jerry Pavia:** 7 top, 29 top, 92, 115, 166, 182; **Victoria Pearson/Getty Images:** 45, 91 top right; **Linda Lamb Peters:** 94 top left, 136; **Garden Pix/Photolibrary:** 171 bottom row #1; **Norm Plate:** 58–59 (design: Troy Bankord), 64–65 (design: Diana Stratton, Diana Stratton Design), 108, 109 left, 113 bottom, 118 (design: Susan Calhoun, Plantswoman Design), 119 (garden design: John Kenyon, Sundance Landscaping), 120; **Matthew Plut:** 178 left (design: Land & Place); **Red Cover/Practical Pictures:** 78 top right; **Red Cover/Ed Reeve:** 48 bottom; **courtesy of Robinson Brick:** 169 bottom row #2; **Lisa Romerein:** 9, 47 bottom, 54 bottom, 176 left, 184, back cover center; **Susan A. Roth:** 89; **Mark Rutherford:** 127 top row #4; **Jeremy Samuelson/Getty Images:** 18 top right, 183 top; **Red Cover/Kim Sayer:** 121; **David Schiff:** 126 top row #1, 127 middle row #4, 127 bottom row

#2; **Christina Schmidhofer:** 49 (design: Davis Dalbok); **Red Cover/Grant Scott:** 186; **JS Sira/ Photolibrary:** 163 bottom right; **Stockbyte/Getty Images:** 127 middle row #2; **Thomas J. Story:** 14–15 (design: Beth Mullins, Growsgreen Landscape Design; construction: Rock & Rose Landscapes), 18 bottom (design: Roberta Walker Landscape Design), 22–23, 34 bottom (design: Michael Manneh and Stefan Offermann), 56 (fire pit design: Perry Becker, Perlman Architects; landscape design: Michael Dollin, Urban Earth Design), 59 top (design: Paul Hendershot Design), 62 (design: Theresa Clark Studio), 78 bottom (design: Ahna Pietras-Dominski), 79, 95, 103 (design: Kappel & Phelps) 107 top, 130, 153 top left, 158 (design: Brian Baird, Scenic Scapes), 159 top left, 159 top middle, 159 top right, 161 all, 173 #3, 177 left, 179 left; **Tim Street-Porter:** 57, 100 top left; **Tim Street-Porter/Getty Images:** 88 bottom, 142; **Dan Stultz:** 125 top right; **E. Spencer Toy:** 132; **Pia Tryde/Getty Images:** 53 top; **Mark Turner:** 17, 54 top left; **Alexander van Berge/Taverne Agency:** 74; **Coral von Zumwalt:** 46–47 (design: Judy Kameon, Michael Kirchmann Jr., and Ivette Soler, Elysian Landscapes); **Dominique Vorillon:** 1, 183 bottom; **Lee Anne White:** 106–107, 112–113 (landscape architect: Richard McPherson); **Lee Anne White/Garden Picture Library/ Photolibrary:** 54 top right; **Michele Lee Willson:** 167 top row #1, 167 top row #2, 169 top row #4; **Katherine Wolkoff/Art + Commerce:** 50; **William Wright:** 18 top left (design: Tish Treherne, Bliss Garden Design), 76–77

Special Thanks

Mark Hawkins, Jeanne Huber, Laura Martin, Brianne McElhiney, Kimberley Navabpour, Marie Pence, Linda Lamb Peters, Alan Phinney, Lorraine Reno, Vanessa Speckman, E. Spencer Toy, Hazel White

index